CONFESSOR COP

THE DETECTIVE WHO PERSUADED KILLERS TO TALK

The life of
CAPTAIN JONATHAN MORRIS
as told to
MICHAEL BEHR

Kwela Books

Cover design: Marthie Steenkamp
Book design: Wilna Combrinck
Editor: Mike Nicol
Proofreader: Christine de Villiers

Originally printed in South Africa
ISBN: 978-0-624-09350-3 (First edition, irst impression 2025)

LSiPOD: 978-0-624-09613-9 (First edition, first impression 2025)

ISBN 978-0-6240-9351-0 (epub)

This is the paradox of the shadow: the very
thing we run from is the doorway into the
very thing we yearn for.
– Michael Brown, author of *The Presence Process*

CONTENTS

PART 1

THE SIZZLERS BOMBSHELL

CHAPTER 1

BREAKING POINT

This is a story about a cop. It's a true story, although at times it doesn't seem like it. At times it seems like a nightmare. The cop's nightmare. His trauma. How he battled with that trauma. How he suppressed it to do his job. How it got him in the end. It's a story about his cop life, and his home life, his wives, his children, his mother. It's the story of Captain Jonathan Morris. I have a photograph of him taking a suspect to court: it's a photograph of the quintessential cop. He's stocky, has close-cropped hair, a broad forehead, set eyes behind wire-frame spectacles, a black moustache over firm lips, a strong chin; he wears a colourful tie, a pale mauve shirt, a shiny, black leather jacket, he's a man with a story. It's a story about what cops have to deal with daily, serious stuff that is sometimes difficult to read. Stuff like this:

It's 4.30am on Monday, 20 January 2003. A phone call jerks Captain Jonathan Morris out of a rare deep sleep.

He answers.

'Môre, môre, Boeta Me!' says Captain Reynold Talmakkies, his Serious and Violent Crimes Unit group leader. 'We need you in Sea Point. Ten men have been shot execution style at a gay massage parlour. It's a big one! Flying squad are waiting for us. Chop-chop. Gou maak!'

Now, two decades later in December 2021, Jonathan's telling me the story. How he's in his old red Toyota, racing from his Mitchells Plain home along deserted roads. Blue light flashing on the dash. Siren blaring. Adrenaline pumping.

It's 4.45am when he swings through the yellow police cordon into Graham Road, Sea Point. Already the street is a scrum of curious onlookers, journalists, and flashing blue and red lights. Jonathan scurries from his car to join his colleagues for a briefing outside number seven. He quickly learns the crime scene is a mess. Flying squad cops have already combed the house for suspects and provided first aid to survivors. Paramedics have come and gone with three survivors. There are bloodied footprints on the carpet, amid a mess of first-aid paraphernalia. They've left behind the gags and ropes they cut from the survivors.

It's not ideal, but chaotic crime scenes have not hindered Jonathan before. What bothers him more is Talmakkies' caution that five victims, still bound and gagged, lie waiting for him in the first room. Their throats have been slit. Blood is congealed around execution style bullet wounds to their heads. In another room, there's a lone victim with similar wounds. Jonathan's been warned: there's a lot of blood in the house. A lot.

'Let's see what we can find,' says Talmakkies, leading the way.

As Jonathan nears the front door, he hears music. Momentarily, it throws him off-kilter. It's the first time he's ever encountered a song, let alone a love ballad, at a murder scene. It's a tune he knows well: Aaron Neville's 'Tell It Like It Is'. It's one of his favourite songs.

Jonathan enters the house, telling himself that after three decades as a violent crime detective in Cape Town, he's seen it all.

But he's dead wrong. Nothing. Not the past decapitations. Not the severed head in a cardboard box. Not the many twisted serial killings. Not the violent gangland slayings. Nothing could have prepared him for the first bedroom on the left.

It comes at him first through his nose. Except this time that all too familiar blood odour swamps him in a sickening, overwhelming wave. Talmakkies wasn't bullshitting, he thinks. This is a lot of blood. And confusingly, it's laced with the smell of petrol.

'It was like walking into a mortuary,' he tells me. 'It smelt like something raw. I can't explain it to you. During my early detective years, we didn't wear masks during autopsies. So, by the time

14

I walked into that room I had done hundreds of them. I knew that smell only too well. It gets up your nose and stays there. But I was used to it. Except this time I nearly vomited. There was blood everywhere. Blood spatter on the walls. The carpet was wet with blood. And the bodies with bulging eyes. Oh my word! Duct tape over the socks in their mouths. Their throats slit. The congealed blood... I kept thinking, who were the monsters who did this? Who could be so fucking cruel?'

There is none of the usual crime scene banter of a first walk-through. No one utters a word. Not even an incredulous, What the fuck! The only sound in the house is Aaron Neville, unfath-omably looping on repeat from an old-fashioned TV.

Down the passage in the next room, there's a white male lying on his side in a pool of blood. In the bloodied bathroom where one of the four miraculous survivors fought his executioner, the paramedics are cleaning up. The man's been rushed to hospital and he's fighting for his life.

Jonathan continues through the house with his five colleagues, dreading what they know comes next. Which is the appointment of the lead detective. To Jonathan's relief it's not him. 'I was som-mer ready to get the hell out of that house,' he tells me. 'Ek wou net dringend uitkom. I mean really urgently.'

Just then a uniformed colleague arrives with the perfect excuse. A witness two blocks down called 10111, saying he saw suspects fleeing the scene around 3am. Jonathan volunteers to interview him and bolts out of the Graham Road slaughterhouse, gulping fresh air to settle his high anxiety. Even now in his retelling his relief is palpable.

It turns out that the eyewitness hasn't much to offer. After hear-ing faint gunshots while dropping off his girlfriend, he saw two guys wearing balaclavas run down the street and get into a white BMW.

After leaving the eyewitness, Jonathan's thoughts turn to his diabetes meds. He needs to take them but only once he's had something to eat. Food is the last thing he wants. But he grabs a sandwich and a coffee from the petrol station opposite the Sea

Point Police Station.

By the time he returns to Sizzlers, his Serious and Violent Crimes Unit commander Brigadier Riaan Booysen has arrived. Pissed off with Talmakkies' decision about the lead detective, he promptly appoints Jonathan lead investigator. Which freaks out Jonathan. How's he going to process this scene on top of the Asanda Baninzi serial killer case involving 18 victims and counting?

'I was already stretched to breaking point.'

But even though every fibre in his body is screaming no, he accepts the order. 'If I get a case I never refuse or complain. I never refused a case in my career.' Professionalism pushes down his fear. 'I knew in my mind, this is a big thing. And there is going to be a lot of pressure. But let's not worry about the pressure. Let me do the basics and make sure that nobody will point a finger. Let me do my best.'

Jonathan doesn't say so, but one gets the sense that he was psyching himself up. Just do the basics. Little steps. Hurry the fuck up so we can get the hell out of this fucking house.

They bag every bit of evidence, Jonathan wondering all the time how much suffering unfolded in those rooms. Wondering who pushed repeat to spoil his favourite song. Wondering whether the killers hated gays.

He doesn't have to do much directing as they process the crime scene. His two-man forensic team is experienced. They document with photos and video as they go. Bagging exhibits. Spraying walls and every other surface with lumina to reveal fingerprints.

By 2pm the mortuary vans have removed the bodies and Jonathan locks the front door.

'I wanted the scene sealed for a week in case, God forbid, I needed to come back. Just for a week then I'm done.'

By now he knows from the eleven 9mm and 7.65mm cartridges found among the bodies on the bloodied carpet that two handguns were used to shoot nine terrified rent boys in the back of their heads. That the one who refused to lie on his stomach was shot in his face. That a pair of kitchen knives were used to slit their throats. That there's a visible fingerprint on the piece of bloodied duct tape cut from the bathroom victim's mouth. He also knows from team members at the hospital that two of the four survivors have since died. That another is in a coma, unlikely to survive the night. And that a fourth is undergoing emergency surgery. He prays this one survives. He also hopes that the special line opened at Sea Point Police Station will yield a lead.

Back in his office later that evening with all the statements taken during the day by team members, Jonathan writes up his investigation diary.

To me he now says that he's exhausted. Indeed, the good detective has been bobbing and weaving my badgering for more detail for almost three hours. It's painstaking because he jumps all over the timeline like a skittish cat.

He is a 'pen and paper guy', he says. He hasn't got a laptop to type all this out. I get the sense that many more hours of interviewing lie in wait. He also tells me that his vivid flashbacks are hard to bear. 'I'm seeing the whole thing again as if it was yesterday.' When pressed, he won't go to the feelings that are surfacing. 'I'm feeling like I'm in court now and you're the defence advocate,' he says with annoyance. We force a laugh but it's clear it's no laughing matter. He says he's almost as exhausted now as he was in 2003 when he got back to his lonely house in the early hours of the morning. 'I had no support structure at home back then. My second marriage of 14 years had fallen apart. She was in the next room but I was geskei van bed en tafel.'

That night the crime scene haunted him. As did the infernal soundtrack looping in his head over, and over, and over again. 'You sleep for an hour or so, and then you're awake, sweating. And I had to be at the mortuary by 9am.

I start interviewing Jonathan over WhatsApp afresh the next day. I push him for more crime scene detail. He remembers but he doesn't want to remember. I have to remind him about details of the case. I email him archive statements to refresh his shattered memory, which previously had been razor sharp. He resists me.

Gets defensive when I point out factual mistakes in his recollections, which are not of the same calibre as the flawless dockets prosecutors knew him for. He tires after another three hours of cross-questioning but promises we can continue the next day.

Can I email him all the documents I have, to refresh his memory?

He's embarrassed – make that ashamed – that he can't accurately recall the sequence of events or some significant dates. It's perfectly understandable after two decades. But Jonathan comes down hard on himself.

Emailing him case documents turns out to be a big mistake.

Over the next few days he dodges my calls. Then his wife collapses and he rushes her to hospital. I don't hear from him until two days before Christmas 2021. It's a bombshell WhatsApp.

'Morning. Tossing and turning. Sweating and can't sleep after reading Quinton's statement. Opening old wounds. I need some space to prepare myself mentally to answer further questions. Going through a tuff time. Hope you'll respectfully accept my request. Don't call me. Thanks. Second night I can't sleep. Dreaming how the victims must've pleaded for their lives. House of horror seems to haunt me after 20 years. I will be comfortable answering further questions when I feel better. Have a blessed day.'

CHAPTER 2

FIRST RESPONDERS

Jonathan and I met in 2004 when I was freelancing as a magazine journalist and was interested in the Sizzlers murders. We talked in his fourth-floor office at the Serious and Violent Crimes Unit in Bishop Lavis about my intention of writing about the Sizzlers murders. I wanted a copy of his Sizzlers docket as I was intrigued by the lack of motive in the murders. But that project never came off the backburner and the docket remained boxed for almost two decades until October 2021.

I was in the offices of NB Publishers, discussing book projects with editor Maryne Lamprecht, when she mentioned that Detective Morris would make a good story. Would I like to follow up?

Yes, I would. It turned out that Captain Jonathan Morris definitely had a book in him. In fact, it had been waiting, he told me, since his retirement. We agreed to do a series of interviews and it was quickly apparent that he had a really good story to tell.

Many of his past investigations would make compelling reading, particularly the high-profile ones. He'd put rapists, murderers and serial killers behind bars. He had kept files on the cases he wanted to talk about. Plus, he had a keen eye for detail and the razor-sharp recall required to bring his cases to life on the page. But what really caught my attention was a unifying theme to his law enforcement. Jonathan had a way of getting criminals to confess. In another life he could have been a priest. Or a therapist.

In those early days of interviewing, I wasn't sure why suspect after suspect confessed to the captain. Then it became clear, his main weapon was his empathetic ear. He intuitively knew exactly which buttons to press when interviewing. 'As soon as I saw tears in a suspect's eyes, I knew his confession was almost on his lips,' he told me.

I was intrigued by the psychology of Jonathan's skill. And as our interviews continued it seemed that we were progressing. We even had the title, Confessor Cop. But then came his Christmas bombshell WhatsApp. There was nothing for it but to wait and hope he would recover.

In the meantime, I sifted through his Sizzlers docket for other impressions of the crime scene. Maybe they would tell me what Jonathan couldn't. I found a statement by Flying Squad Captain Jacobus Naude, the first cop through the front door. Jonathan would have only read it that evening while writing up Day 1 of his investigation diary. It was anything but bedtime reading.

Naude and two flying squad colleagues are patrolling Sea Point, when bystanders at the Total garage in Main Road flag them down. There, sitting on the step at the garage shop, they find a man covered in blood. While radioing for an ambulance, an hysterical man approaches the squad car, screaming at Naude that he's stumbled on a bloodbath.

The bewildered captain calms him down. The man's name is Mark Hamilton, a Sizzlers regular. Normally he rings the bell at 7 Graham Road, but this time he found the security gate ajar. At about 3.30am he stepped inside, he tells Naude. Looking into the room to his left, he saw blood everywhere, bodies lying next to each other on the floor. Instead of turning and running, Hamilton was drawn to the bloodied knife on the passage table. Picking it up, he glanced to his right into the private room of the massage parlour owner. The cupboards were open, their contents strewn about. Yet still he walked deeper into the heart of darkness. In the second room to his left there was a man lying on the floor, wet blood pooled around his head. Only then did Hamilton come to his senses. Leaving the knife on the table, he fled Sizzlers, running down the street to the garage.

Rattled by Hamilton's account, Naude calls for backup. Then he races to Sizzlers with Hamilton, followed by a Sea Point patrol car that had arrived at the garage. Instructing Hamilton to stay put, Naude enters the dimly lit house at 3.45am to search for suspects. His account is much the same as Jonathan's except for the six men lying next to one another in a 'neat row' on a bloodied carpet. They're bound hand and foot with brown tape gagging their mouths. All are lying on their stomachs, their faces turned to the right. Naude can tell some are still alive because they're gurgling. Their eyes are open. And they are also jerking. He resists the urge to help until he's sure there are no suspects lurking in the shadows.

The room to his right is also a mess. And he notices the telephone is off the hook. Moving to the next room to his left, the captain finds a bound man, hole in his head, throat slit, lying in his own blood. He has no doubt this one is dead. Further down the passage he encounters a bound older man in a bathroom slippery wet with blood. His throat is horribly slit and blood is still pumping from his body. This one is definitely alive.

Throughout his search Naude fights the impulse to silence the poodle running around barking its head off.

Mark Hamilton meanwhile re-enters the house, even though he'd been told to remain outside. He tries to speak to one survivor in the first room. But he's gagged and drowning in his own blood. Hamilton spins round to what sounds like snoring from behind the bed at the window.

As Naude comes back into the room, Hamilton tells him that there's someone behind the bed. Naude tips the bed and finds a seventh victim barely alive, also drowning in his own blood behind his gag. Despite his injuries, blood smudges suggest he managed to roll under the bed to escape further harm.

Turning back to the room, Naude notices for the first time the many bullet casings lying in a lot of blood.

Confident that Sizzlers is now secure, he and fellow officers cut the ropes binding the survivors' hands and feet, and the duct tape from their mouths so that they can breathe again. Then they apply basic first aid until the first paramedics rush into the room at 4am.

By the time Naude departs the horror at 5.35am, Sizzlers is crawling with detectives and forensic investigators. And all the survivors he helped save have been rushed to hospital.

I get the picture: rent boys pleading for their lives as their throats are slit – not to kill them outright, but just enough to strike fear into them. Their muffled panic as petrol is sprinkled over them. Then multiple gunshots to the head at point blank range. A fight to the death with a client who stopped having sex in the second room to investigate the disturbing noises outside.

Surely the neighbours heard something? I find just one statement in Jonathan's docket.

It's a short account from a German tourist in a nearby bed-and-breakfast who was woken about 15 minutes before Hamilton arrived at Sizzlers, and it makes bizarre reading.

'I woke up because of a strange sound. It almost sound like somebody got strangled. The person wanted to yell or to make a sound, but it sounded like the person couldn't. A few moments later I heard a shot followed by three or four other shots. I couldn't see anything but I was sure it could be gunshots. Then there was a little pause, and I heard at least four or five shots more. It sounded like the last couple of shots were in another room or location. It sounded a little different, so I thought that the second sequence took place in another location. I did not notice any arguing. There might have been some but I did not hear anything because I could be asleep. I did not hear any footsteps running or motor cars after the incident. I might have fallen asleep after this because the next thing I heard was police sirens and I saw the blue lights.'

It's dumbfounding how anyone could have dozed through the attack. In the docket's crime scene photos is the graphic evidence of what still freaks out Jonathan. For a long time, I've avoided these brutally candid snapshots. But with Jonathan out of action there's no escape. It's what he wanted me to do.

'You want to get a feel of what I went through?' he had snapped more than once during what he likes to call my interrogation. 'Then go feel the photos.'

In truth they are sickening. They prompt a million whys. A deep despondency. Feelings of dread. They reek of brutality. And a quiet rage. They cry out with helplessness.

The four bodies lying alongside one another in the centre of the room were dead when Naude went back to tend to the survivors. You can tell because they are still gagged. Police photographers clearly took these photographs after the living had been rushed to hospital.

The brown duct tape is wrapped so tightly around the socks bulging from their dead mouths that all must have thought they were suffocating. While their hearts raced in anticipation of a bullet to the head. It's hard to make out their bloodied expressions framed against their still glistening blood halos on the carpet. If anything, there's a hint of resignation to the inevitability of the moment. Each body has an A4 sheet of paper tucked between its legs. Declarations of death placed there by paramedics who had found no vitals.

The camera then shifts to the youngster Naude found underneath the window once he had upturned the pine bed. In a close-up, the ginger-headed lad could be sleeping were it not for his bloodied head and gaping throat wound. His arm is resting quietly on his chest as if he is beckoning to someone. Not in desperation but in grace.

The room is a mess of strewn belongings. It tells a story of disgusting work conditions. These boys bled out onto carpets filthy with years of deep stains. Their hand-me-down linen looks like it hasn't been washed for months. Even before the massacre, the room must have smelt bad. These boys had slept on dirty mattresses on bunk beds that give the room the appearance of an overcrowded communal jail cell. One bunk is a double. The other is four tiers high.

The ceiling bears witness to the moment the massage parlour owner's carotid was severed. Cones mark the positions of bullet cartridges. Except for the bizarrely placed bottle of tomato sauce suggesting the forensic team must have run out of cones.

The second room tells a similar story as the first, except there's a double bed covered in a grubby pink-and-blue floral duvet that screams, washing machine. Lubricant, a condom wrapper and a discarded condom on the stained beige carpet suggest other priorities.

No wonder Jonathan wanted to get the hell out of the house. No wonder he resisted being dragged through the front door again even if it was just in his imagination.

I held off contacting him until mid-January 2022, then messaged him again via WhatsApp.

'You opened up old wounds,' he snapped. 'Your advokaating rattled me. (Advokaating is what he calls my interviewing technique.) I felt like I was in the dock being grilled by a defence advocate.' By asking questions I was apparently pushing him back into the crime scene and he didn't want to go there. 'You understand what I'm saying?'

Later 'advokaat' became Jonathan's safe word when questions got too close to the bone.

'I want to be finished with the Sizzlers crime scene. I want to move on to my other cases. Being in the crime scene, to see it again, it's like a house of horrors. Thinking how they must have suffered, screaming for help and being drenched with petrol. It's almost like I was part and parcel of that crime scene again. You understand what I'm trying to say?'

'I understand that, Jonathan, but your first-hand recollection needs to be in your book. I can't just rehash dockets and court files,' I said, thinking that I might be forced to.

Jonathan said he understood, but I was not convinced. He added that he was angry when he WhatsApped me. Angry with me and the perpetrators of the Sizzlers killings. But he was okay to continue with his book.

I told him I thought he had post-traumatic stress disorder that needed treatment. He told me he was treated in November 2014, after 37 years of service. The trigger was a minor text message disagreement with a senior officer about overstepping his authority.

'I stripped my moer and left the scene. If he was standing in front of me, I think I would've killed him.'

'Stripped my moer' was one of his favourite sayings. In ordinary language it means he got seriously angry.

Jonathan returned to work a couple of days later but didn't last long. Following a panic attack in the office, colleagues bundled him over the road to a Melomed Hospital.

'I explained the situation to a doctor in the emergency room. He told me I was a time-bomb.'

The next day Jonathan was admitted to a private psychiatric clinic for three weeks. After just two weeks of individual sessions involving no trauma therapy, he was discharged early with the advice that it was time to retire. It took him another two years before he finally threw in the towel.

'I couldn't handle it any more.'

Four decades of trauma needed more than two weeks treatment, I responded, reminding him how he described his time in the clinic. That it was more a case-by-case debriefing than actual trauma therapy.

'I'm pretty sure that if I take you back into the Sizzlers house, it's going to trigger you all over again,' I said. 'If it was just a one-off thing, you would have phoned me back fast and said, let's go.' Jonathan reluctantly agreed.

I continued: 'You haven't reached out to me. And I deliberately left you alone to see when you would come back and you didn't come back. The only thing that's prompted this conversation is our book contracts that we have to sign this month. If we sign and you relapse, we won't meet the contract's tight deadline. And I'm not prepared to take that risk.'

Jonathan confirmed he wanted to finish the book.

'I need to put this on paper for my grandchildren so they can see what their grandfather went through and achieved in his career. I also want people to understand the sacrifices I've made.'

This was not just about the book, I explained, my patience wearing thin. 'I'm not prepared to go ahead until you've had therapy. I'm saying this so that your grandchildren are left with a legacy and a grandfather who is emotionally whole, who they can still talk to. That's more important than any book.'

'I think I'm fine. But I'll keep that in mind.'

'How about just going for an assessment?'

'You know what they say, cowboys don't cry. And now you want this cowboy to cry? I think I'm fine.'

I gave it two days before calling Jonathan again. He hadn't made a therapy appointment. But he acknowledged the likelihood of being triggered again. And he saw the dangers in signing a contract that would accelerate his time-bomb.

'We can stop now,' he said. 'But what I'm gonna do is call you when I'm really, really over this whole thing. I'm gonna collect the material, all the dockets and statements I can find, so I can refresh my memory. I will also try write my feelings down. And then when I feel better, then I'll give you a call. Just give me time to sort myself out.'

I have a million questions about Sizzlers alone. But Jonathan gave me no choice. I let him go, not knowing if I would ever hear from him again.

CHAPTER 3

LAPTOP THERAPY

I knew something of Jonathan's story from drafting his memoir pitch to the publishers in 2021. I've also pieced together a fair amount from the dockets and court files. I'm trying to move ahead in Jonathan's absence. This may well be the only way to complete his book. Once he treats his trauma, we can always come back and embellish these chapters.

I give Jonathan a couple of months to sort himself out. When he doesn't call, I WhatsApp him.

'I'm coping,' he replies.

His doctor has advised against restarting his book project until he's certain he can stay the distance. Otherwise, he risks a traumatic relapse. He's happy we didn't sign our book contracts.

'Now there's no pressure, né?'

'When do you think you'll be ready?'

'I'll let you know.'

Two months pass before I break silence again in June 2022. Jonathan has just returned from a two-week Namibian holiday and another up the West Coast. He sounds lighter.

'Since I'm back, I'm just at home. I'm teaching myself to use a laptop. It keeps my mind occupied.'

I'm surprised. Throughout his career Jonathan avoided computers.

'I would always hit the wrong knoppie [key] when I tried to type a statement. And that would just make me confused. If I made a mistake while I was writing, I would just scratch it out. And then get someone to type it for me when I was finished.'

Whatever he's working on he's not saying.

Several months later I call again. I learn that instead of seeking therapy, Jonathan is calming himself by typing out his old cases, strolling through his past investigations, keystroke by keystroke.

'I'm enjoying myself,' he says.

When he wakes at 2am, instead of tossing and turning with the violent memories that keep sleep at bay, Jonathan now rises.

'I'm just typing and typing. And if I'm finished with one chapter, I feel so good. I don't feel any trauma any more. I'm just relaxed. I think I will finish by the end of this year.'

But he's not rushing it, which is therapeutic in itself.

'If I feel like doing it, I sit. If I don't want to, then I don't want to.'

Jonathan has so taken to his newfound process that he is writing night and day. And, almost counterintuitively, he is watching true crime TV.

'It gives me new ideas and helps me remember. Then I go back to my cases and make changes.'

But early morning remains Jonathan's favourite creative time.

'When I start at 2am, time just flies. The next thing I know it's 5am. It's nice. I should have taught myself to type a long time ago.'

His search for old dockets from his past cases is proving challenging, however. SAPS usually destroys dockets after 20 years. So he's calling old contacts in prosecutors' offices and police stations. He's not as pushy as I'd like him to be, but pushiness was never his thing, especially when it came to getting a quick confession.

'I'm a funny guy. If I asked you once or twice and you don't respond, I sommer leave it. I'm not going to force my way.'

Clearly his new rituals have dialled down his nightmares. It's helping with recall and sorting out the chronology of his investigations. By the sounds of things, it's doubtful whether a therapist could have prescribed a better path to wellness.

But Sizzlers still haunts him. Particularly telling it like it is.

'I keep thinking why was that song playing when the killers entered the room? Did they choose it? If so, why? Why play it over and over? It's still something I want to explore one day because during my investigation this sort of thing was the last thing on my mind. But this bugs me now.'

Sizzlers, he agrees, is still a roadblock to getting his memoir back on track.

'But I'll get there. Because I just want to get it out the way and never think about Sizzlers again.'

Is therapy the key? I keep that thought to myself. Best not rock Jonathan's lifeboat.

The following year, in March 2023, I contact him again. A Christmas has come and gone since Jonathan's bombshell WhatsApp and I'm wondering why he has been so silent about sorting himself out. Thankfully he appears to be more upbeat. Not ready to return to the book interviews, but still typing away furiously. In addition to his typing habit, another behavioural change is keeping his lifeboat on an even keel.

'Usually, I would discuss my cases with friends. They expected that. The only way I could talk with them was as a cop. But once I started typing, I kept my war stories between me and my computer. Somehow not talking about the skop, skiet and donner quietened things down in my head. So now I don't discuss my cases any more. If friends ask, I just tell them to wait for my book.'

He can't resist the sarcastic comment that we should get a move on: 'So ons beter gou maak, né?'

I let it slide because we both know he hasn't started therapy.

Jonathan changes the subject and our conversation drifts into just how much personal stress he was under during his Sizzlers investigation. I wonder if perhaps these unresolved relationship emotions compounded his triggering over Christmas 2021. There had been the ending of his second marriage, but now he adds his mother to the details.

'I'm not brave at all when it comes to sharing my private life.'

Actually, it's like pulling teeth, but slowly he opens up.

Jonathan met his second wife in the late-1980s when they were both 30. By then he was a detective sergeant at Mitchells Plain Police Station, where she was an admin clerk.

'We dated for two years, then she fell pregnant. We got married in 1990, when our son was three.'

It's an awkward conversation.

What was the attraction?

'Lust.'

It sounds like you were reluctant to marry?

'Yes.'

Relationship issues piled up over the years, but the deal breaker was a rejection of Jonathan's two daughters from his first marriage who were eight and 10 at the time.

'I had a close relationship with my daughters and wanted to see them as often as I could. We went on regular outings and spent time together with my family. My new wife didn't want to be part of that. It hurt me. So I kept my children and my new wife apart.'

There's a long pause. Deep sadness breaks his silence.

'I was married 14 years to that woman. Fourteen wasted years.'

Not entirely so, he later confesses once his regret has subsided.

The silver lining was his son, who was 14 at the time of Jonathan's 2004 divorce and living with his mother in Mitchells Plain.

'We had a good relationship and it's still as strong as before. I love all my children equally, and they adore me.'

By the time Sizzlers engulfed his life, marriage counselling was not an option.

'The situation was so broken. We were long past our sell-by date. Divorce was a relief for us both, as we knew there was nothing left to retrieve. We both were not perfect. It was time to move on.'

While still wrapping up the Sizzlers case, Jonathan moved out of his marital home in April 2003 to live with his 74-year-old mother. It brought much-needed stability and support to his life, especially during a drawn-out divorce, which was only finalised in September 2004.

Were you happier?

'I got my meals on time and did not have to do my own washing. I was free to come and go. And my friends and family were welcome at any time. It was an ubuntu house.'

Jonathan spent nearly a decade living the single life and being a dedicated father. 'I spent most of my time with my children and grandchildren. And I had a side chick, but nothing serious.'

Ever the ladies' man, Jonathan also spent nearly a decade as a single cop after his first divorce.

What was the attraction when you met your first wife?

'She was hot.'

The marriage lasted eight years.

'I had an affair.'

In 2010, while still living with his mother, Jonathan started dating Leonore Marinus, a 55-year-old widow and ex-neighbour who regularly visited Jonathan's mother and sister. Jonathan was now 52 years old.

'It was our secret for a couple of years until somebody exposed us! It was a big joke and fun to date secretly.'

What was the attraction of this mother of four?

'She was the one. It was true love. She accepted me for who I am with all my baggage.'

His baggage included a chequered past, which was only revealed in our later discussions when he confessed. 'Before I joined the police I had two sons out of wedlock. I don't like to talk about my private life. It's not easy admitting that I made mistakes with women in my younger years. I'm not proud of it. But it's part of me. After thinking about it, it's not something I can scratch out of my story.'

I can't help wondering what else he's scratched out because of shame. What else is Jonathan hiding about his past?

Jonathan concludes our March 2023 call with an unexpected Sizzlers twist. Towards the end of 2022 he posed for photos with his grandkids outside 7 Graham Road.

'They always asked me about my work and wanted to know if Pa was a good cop. And they had heard of the Sizzlers case from their mom and dad. So while we were in Sea Point one day, I said, come, I'll show you the house. It looked very different, with big fat plants in the garden. They got excited and bombarded me with questions. I had to show them where the getaway car was parked and the flat where one of the killers must have watched the comings and goings from the house. They told me they were very proud of Grandpa and asked me about my book. Then I got tired and decided to leave.'

Jonathan doesn't say he's ready for us to delve into the Sizzlers case file again. He hasn't started therapy. But returning to the crime scene is surely a sign he could be close?

Come mid-2023, Jonathan is still typing up a storm. Miraculously, the process has revealed why he is a trauma time-bomb.

'I don't know if I call it insomnia. But this laptop is keeping me busy. When I can't sleep, I'm going through my case files and just go on typing and typing,' he tells me. 'It's opened up a lot of things. Stuff that I really blocked out.'

The realisation occurred when Jonathan's cousin and son-in-law – his main pillars of support during his days in the Serious and Violent Crimes Unit – became curious about his voracious keyboard habit. How the hell did you survive the horror, they asked when they saw what he was typing.

'I was typing one night when the answer hit me. When I was finished with a crime scene, I dreamt about it for a few nights. Then you know how I blocked my cases out? Because there was another one, and another one, and another one. That is how I dealt with my past and coped with the trauma. Do you understand what I'm saying? Every time it's a new one. I couldn't understand that back then. But the more I typed, I realised I was on a conveyor belt. Everybody got a week off after being on standby. But every time I'm on standby, then I get a new case. Sometimes my colleagues would go weeks working on their case without getting a new one.

But I was getting a new case almost every week. Sometimes I had three cases open at the same time. That is what happened. And that's how I survived because every time it's just a new case. I now see that if I had time off and time to think about the cases and dwell on them, I don't think I would've survived for so many years.'

It's a startling epiphany that seems to liberate Jonathan. His workaholism was a brilliant, unconscious survival strategy. He basically blocked the trauma of one case with the trauma of another. Case after case he never dealt with the pain of being exposed to so much violence and depravity. Until finally at the last hurdle of his career he fell down.

Why didn't he just take time off? Why did his superiors have to force him to take his leave?

'I was taught by the old detectives, if you get a new case, work it bliksem hard in the first week till you crack it, then you can take it easy for the rest of the month. But there wasn't that leeway at Serious Crimes and I just carried on with my old way. When I solved a case the next one was there, and the next and the next. I remember one day I had three cases on trial at the High Court. I'd sit in court for an hour, then go to the next court for an hour to see if everything is going smoothly, and the next. And I had to testify in each one. That's how I rolled.'

CHAPTER 4

SIX IN A ROW

Jonathan takes almost two years to sort himself out. Not with trauma therapy but with hours of contemplation and keyboard time.

Soon after his mid-2023 realisation that workaholism was his trauma coping strategy, we return cautiously to his Sizzlers investigation. It's 8am, the day after the massacre. Jonathan is at the Salt River Mortuary. He hated the mortuary. But he forced himself through the door because this was where the dead whispered their tortured secrets and he needs all the help he can get. Two of his potential eyewitnesses are dead. He has no crime scene leads. He's pinning his hopes on the remaining two survivors fighting for their lives in Groote Schuur Hospital.

It doesn't look good.

Gregory Berghaus, the 44-year-old punter who bravely fought with his attacker, is barely alive in ICU after surgery to repair a gunshot wound to his stomach. Plus a craniotomy to relieve the massive swelling caused by a bullet still lodged in his brain.

The 25-year-old sex worker Quinton Taylor is also hanging by a thread in ICU with bullet wounds to his neck and jaw.

Jonathan is thankful to be greeted by state pathologist Dr Lorna Martin, who has worked on dozens of his cases over the years. He trusts her.

Her friendly presence quells his rising panic as the six bodies come into view. There's no blood yet. And there seems to be something absurdly calming about the way their peaceful shapes are lined up next to one other in a neat, quiet, white row. But Jonathan has been here before. In the moment that first sheet is peeled back, the nightmare of the previous day will return.

Again there's yesterday's smell of blood. Except this morning it tastes different on Jonathan's tongue. Here it's laced not with petrol but the unforgettable smell of human flesh. Coupled with the sounds and sights to his left, it's enough to send the bravest soul screaming for the exit.

'It sounded like a construction site,' he tells me, recalling the cutting team in full swing. Hacksawing though crowns of heads to remove brains. Power-sawing down the midline to pare the corpses like spatchcock chickens in preparation for the post-mortem. Intestines popping out of body cavities. Blood everywhere on stainless steel tops and white tiles.

'You never get used to it, no matter how many years on the job.' It didn't matter that he'd witnessed hundreds of autopsies. To watch six in a row on one day and then two more the next was a bridge too far. 'I don't think anybody will be able to do that. Will you be able to do that?'

His question was mildly confrontational, as if to say, you have no fucking idea what I went through.

Today Jonathan has to suppress his instinctual urge to flee six fold. 'I had to push the fear down hard. Your attendance is of utmost importance. I'm there to assist the pathologist with what transpired on the crime scene. To campaign for the dead.'

Jonathan's first visit to a mortuary was in 1980 as a rookie detective. 'The smell of human flesh was horrific and stayed with me for weeks. The pathologist would make sure that you watched your first post-mortem until the end. It was part of your initiation. After that I couldn't go into a butchery for months because the smell reminded me of the mortuary. I eventually got used to it. I found a way to fight the urge to throw up and run so I could carry out my duties. Vicks. Plenty of Vicks up the nose does the trick.'

But today nothing can quieten the charnel house chatter in Jonathan's head. In the absence of a first-hand account, it's doing an excellent job imagining how the massacre unfolded. With great effort born of experience, Jonathan bookmarks his thoughts and feelings. This is not about him. Post-mortem is about justice for the brothers, sisters, sons and daughters behind death register numbers.

Sergio De Castro, 22 years old
DR [Death Register] 149/2003
Chief post-mortem findings:
4.1. The body of a young adult male with a perforating gunshot wound to the face, that exits above the right ear.
4.2. A deep penetrating incision to the left side of the neck that incises muscles.
4.3. Ligature abrasions to the left wrist and both ankles.
4.4. Lacerating gunshot wound tract to the brain, with subdural and subarachnoid bleeding over the brain.
Cause of death: Gunshot wound of the brain.

Timothy Craig Boyd, 29 years old
DR 150/2003
Chief post-mortem findings:
4.1. The body of a young adult male with a single perforating gunshot wound to the back of the head that exits out of the right eye.
4.2. There are three stab wounds to the back of the neck that incise the muscles of the neck.
4.3. There are ligature abrasions around both ankles and the right wrist.
4.4. There is a lacerating gunshot wound tract through the brain, with subdural and subarachnoid bleeding.
Cause of death: Gunshot wound of the brain.

Aubrey John Otgaar, 56 years old
DR 151/2003
Chief post-mortem findings:
4.1. The body of a middle-aged male with two perforating gunshot wounds to the back of the head, that exit over the left forehead.
4.2. A large gaping incised wound to the left side of neck that incises muscles, the carotid artery and the pharynx.
4.3. Two lacerating gunshot wound tracks through the brain that fracture the skull, with subarachnoid bleeding over the brain.
4.4. A ligature abrasion around the right wrist.
4.5. Multiple contusions to the upper arms and abrasion, consistent with a bite, over the right shoulder.
Cause of death: Gunshot wounds of the brain.

Johan Joseph Meyer, 20 years old
DR 152/2003
Chief post-mortem findings:
4.1. Adult male.
4.2. Gunshot wound of the back of the head with a wound tract that involved the brain.
4.3. Gunshot wound of the right side of the neck with a wound tract that involved the right internal jugular vein.
Cause of death: Gunshot wounds of the head and neck.

Travis Reade, 20 years old
DR 153/2003
Chief post-mortem findings:
4.1. Adult male.
4.2. Entrance gunshot wound of the left side of the head with a wound tract that involved the brain.
4.3. Superficial penetrating incised wounds of the neck.
Cause of death: Gunshot wound of the head.

Stephanus Abraham Fouche, 17 years old

DR 154/2003.

Chief post-mortem findings:

4.1. Male juvenile.

4.2. Gunshot wound at the back of the head with a wound tract that involved brain.

4.3. Superficial penetrating incised wounds of the neck.

Cause of death: Gunshot wound of the head.

Warren Robert Visser, 22 years old

DR 159/2003

Chief post-mortem findings:

4.1. The body of a young adult male with a single perforating gunshot wound to the right temple that exits over the left scalp.

4.2. There is a lacerating gunshot wound tract through the brain, with subdural and subarachnoid bleeding over the brain.

4.3. There are three sutured incised wounds to the neck that incise muscles, one of which enters the right posterior chest cavity.

4.4. There are ligature imprints around the wrist and ankles.

Cause of death: A gunshot wound of the brain.

Marius Meyer, 21 years old

DR 171/2003

Chief post-mortem findings:

4.1. Body of a young adult male with a perforating gunshot wound to the left temporal region of the scalp that exits over the right temple.

4.2. There are three sutured incised wounds to the neck that incise muscles.

4.3. There is a lacerating gunshot wound tract through the brain, with subdural and subarachnoid haemorrhage and brain swelling.

4.4. There are ligature abrasions on the ankles.

Causes of death: Gunshot wound of the brain.

Gregory Seymour Berghaus, 44 years old
DR 192/2003
Chief post-mortem findings:

4.1. The body of an adult male with a perforating gunshot wound to the left temple that exits over the back of the head.
4.2. There is a gunshot wound tract through the left cerebrum with marked necrosis, infarction of the brain and swelling.
4.3. There is evidence that a craniotomy has been performed.
4.4. There is a penetrating gunshot wound tract to the abdomen that lacerates the small bowel and the appendix.
4.5. There is a sutured incised wound to the neck that incises the sterno-cleidomastoid muscle.
4.6. There are ligature imprints/abrasions around the wrists.

Cause of death: A gunshot wound of the brain.

Post-mortem is also when family arrive at the mortuary to identify their loved ones. To claim their bodies. And hopefully hear something from the investigating officer that will put their minds at rest.

'I still remember the sadness and helpless I felt meeting the fathers of Stephanus Fouche and Marius Meyer,' Jonathan tells me over WhatsApp. Both fathers had requested their sons' bodies be released late so that they could drive them back home in the cool of the night. 'All I could promise them was that I would do my best to solve the case and find justice for their children.'

Jonathan couldn't recall their first names. Only that Mr Fouche was from Theunissen in the Free State and didn't say much. But he vividly remembered the words of Mr Meyer, an ex-cop from Kimberley.

'Morris, my friend, this is going to be a very difficult case for you. There's going to be a lot of pressure. Good luck.'

Both fathers were shocked that their sons had been sex workers.

'All they knew was their sons had gone to work in Cape Town. They had no clue what type of work.'

Jonathan spared them the terrifying truth of eight autopsies.

'Once their slit throats were cleaned, you could see just how gruesome the wounds were. It's like hate and rage jumped out at me as Lorna did her work. Those boys must have suffered. This was torture. I don't remember that I ever investigated a case where torture was involved.'

When I ask Jonathan about his feelings that day, he struggles to remember. 'It was emotional.'

What do you mean?

'I had to pull myself together.'

How do you mean?

'I felt really sad. But I had a job to do.'

When Gregory Berghaus died four days later in ICU, Dr Martin sensed Jonathan couldn't stomach any more. 'She just sommer excused me from the last post-mortem. She knew I was stretched to breaking point.'

Stretched also because he had no early leads.

This was the biggest case of his life. The media were all over it, baying for answers while fuelling speculation that the Sizzlers massacre was a homophobic hate crime or part of a gang turf war. And all Jonathan had was Quinton, the youngster Captain Naude found sitting in his own blood on the step of the garage shop.

By some miracle he was still in intensive care. Would he live long enough to talk? Would he even remember with two bullets still lodged in his head?

CHAPTER 5

THE GAME CHANGER

Normally it took Jonathan 48 hours to get a confession. But Sizzlers was his game changer. By Day 4 of his investigation he had nothing. Nothing except an unfamiliar rising sense of dread that he had lost his touch.

Jonathan thought his luck had turned when a fingerprint was lifted from Berghaus's duct-tape gag. Until forensics found the print belonged to Berghaus. Before he passed out on the bathroom floor, he must have feebly reached up to pull the suffocating gag from his mouth.

When Berghaus died in ICU on Day 5, Jonathan knew his investigation was in trouble. Quinton was his last chance.

But doctors were not letting Jonathan near his ICU bed. Quinton was stable but still in a critical condition. His jaw had been fractured by a bullet that was still lodged there, and his throat had been cut. That was sewn up but he still couldn't speak. There was a second bullet lodged in his neck, where it had come to rest after fracturing the base of his skull. And he was hooked up to a ventricular drainage system to reduce the build-up of fluid in his swollen brain.

'The waiting was the worst part,' recalled Jonathan in earlier interviews that captured the detective's mounting anxiety. 'I couldn't wait to get to Quinton to get my breakthrough.'

It came on Friday, 25 January, the same day Berghaus was declared brain dead and disconnected from his ventilator.

'When I walked into his private ward, I was shocked by Quinton's appearance,' said Jonathan.' The pipes, his swollen eyes, his bullet wounds, his shaved head. He looked bad. I had to steady myself because it was like it was one of those boys on the floor had risen from the dead.

Quinton barely nodded when I introduced myself as the investigating officer.

'The first thing I asked him was how many killers were in the house. He held up two fingers. That first meeting was over quick. The nurse told me I'd get more out of Quinton if I came back in two days' time.'

The waiting was unbearable. Jonathan knew every day was a day wasted. And his nerves weren't coping.

'I couldn't sleep. My head just kept turning and turning with flashbacks of the crime scene and the mortuary. I could hear how the victims pleaded for their lives while being tortured. And the perpetrators still roamed the streets.'

Day 2: Sunday, 26 January 2003

'The nurse was right. Quinton managed a few words but I could see it wasn't easy for him. And it was hard for me to understand what he was trying to tell me. But I was over the moon. I spent an hour with him, making notes as he described the horror. Then he got anxious and I had to stop the interview. I was patient. I didn't want to push him and blow it. I told him to relax and that together we would bring the killers to book. I promised to be back the next day.'

Day 3: Monday, 27 January 2003

'I continued with my notes and after an hour I was interrupted by a grumpy ward sister who reprimanded me for disturbing her patient. I reminded her that she was interfering with my duties. Then I decided to leave before saying something I would regret. Quinton told me not to worry and that he looked forward to seeing me the next day.'

Jonathan followed the same daily routine that week. First he attended his morning briefing at the office, where he updated his commander about his progress with Quinton. Then he drove down to Grand West Casino for his 'stress reliever': an hour on the five-cent slot machines.

He began this self-therapy after his first divorce and found it very effective. 'It took my mind off everything.'

Did he ever hit the jackpot?

'The only machine that ever paid out to me was the ATM.'

Day 4: Tuesday, 28 January 2003

Jonathan's anxieties rose when he spotted a pair of SAPS Crime Intelligence Unit goons lurking near Quinton's ward. He immediately recognised them from the day before at his Bellville offices, where they were ordered to stay away from his chief witness.

'It was two white guys. Two captains. I asked them, what's going on? With their Security Branch attitude they told me they had received information that Quinton was a liar. He was involved with the perpetrators and they were here to interrogate him. And that they would remove his medical pipes to force him to tell the truth. I called my commander and they disappeared. I never saw them again. But it took a while for me to calm down. If I hadn't spotted them, they would have messed up my case. They came there with their apartheid attitudes. I've never trusted intelligence cops because they're not so intelligent. They were acting on rumours flying around in the media. The stories that the Fast Guns or other gangs were involved and wanting to take Quinton out were bullshit. How could Quinton be involved? He took two bullets to the head and was fighting for his life and they come with this rubbish.

'I didn't want anybody to interfere. I had Quinton just where I wanted him – calm, trusting me and cooperating with me. He was my only lead and these monkeys wanted to barge in and fuck everything up. All my patience with Quinton would have been down the drain. I was the moer in.

'After that I informed the nurses that nobody was allowed to see Quinton except me.

'He was pleased to see me. I told him the story and that he only talks to me. Thirty minutes later Quinton became tired and asked me to leave. He needed to sleep. As I left, he asked me to bring cigarettes and a Coke the next day.'

Day 5: Wednesday, 29 January 2003

'I was back the following day with cigarettes and Coke *and* a chocolate. Quinton was happy and we continued with my questions. We were in a good space and trusted each other.'

Day 6: Thursday, 30 January 2003

'I continued taking notes while Quinton drank his Coke. By the end of the day I had all I needed. I told him I'd be back with the statement over the weekend. He was happy because his parents were coming to visit.'

Day 7: Sunday, 2 February 2003

'It was short and sweet. All Quinton needed to do was read his statement and sign. As I left, I told him I'd be back to fetch him when he was discharged.'

Most of the Jonathan's questions had been answered. While eight of the sex workers were watching a gangster movie, two killers, masquerading as clients, had entered their quarters shortly after midnight with the owner Eric, whom they seemed to know. Instead of choosing a rent boy, they drew guns and then robbed the boys and Eric of their jewellery and cash.

The victims were then ordered to lie on their stomachs to be bound and gagged. Except Quinton, who refused, telling the killers: 'If I'm gonna die, I want to see it coming.'

Jonathan also heard how the boys cried in fear as the killers stabbed them and cut their throats. And then how, after being splashed with petrol, they were shot in the head at point blank range, one by one.

Jonathan was grateful for the miracle that had kept Quinton alive. He had a lot more to go on than a week ago. Not just a vivid account of the nightmare on Graham Road but a detailed description of the killers.

The downside was his perfect eyewitness had never seen them before.

Jonathan's last remaining option was to put as many mugshot books in front of Quinton as he could. But that would mean doing a tour of police stations with him, which was out of the question right now. Quinton was still in ICU and due for surgery to remove the bullets. Without the motivation of a breakthrough the detective had to dig deep. He'd complete the investigation for the inquest. He'd close every loophole so none of his superiors could point fingers at him. And then hope that one day somebody would get caught with one of the Sizzlers massacre guns.

CHAPTER 6

RESURRECTION

Quinton's miraculous discharge two days after he signed his statement took Jonathan by surprise. But he wasted no time. He wanted to finish with him quickly so he could focus on the other dockets on his desk.

After picking Quinton up at Groote Schuur Hospital, he drove straight to Sea Point Police Station, where the docket had been opened. From there they'd move to mugshot books at Woodstock. But as perky as he looked, Jonathan doubted Quinton would last that long.

He handed the business of going through the mugshot books to his colleague Detective Inspector Deon de Villiers.

'I wanted Quinton to go through them with De Villiers so that I didn't influence his choice in any way. Sometimes when you build a relationship with a witness they try to please you. I wanted this process to run like an ID parade, which the investigating officer is not allowed to attend.'

Quinton looked at two current mugshot books of about 500 photos but drew a blank. Before packing it in, admin clerk Anna Louw suggested she fetch old black-and-white albums they no longer used from the archives. Flipping through the first dusty album, Quinton halted abruptly on Photo 2899. It was one of the shooters.

Jonathan wasn't convinced by the photo De Villiers showed him. It was more than 12 years old. The man looking back at him appeared to be anything but a cold-blooded killer. And he was small fry. His crime in the album index read: use of a motor vehicle without the owner's consent.

'Are you sure?' Jonathan asked Quinton.

Covering the forehead and chin of the scruffy-looking man so that just his eyes were visible, Quinton nodded. 'I'll never forget those eyes. They were watching us the whole time.'

Normally, these words would have pleased Jonathan but he didn't want to get his hopes up. His witness was fresh out of ICU with two bullets still lodged in his head. His brain needed someone to pin the blame on and had found it in a dusty mugshot book.

Sceptically, he noted the suspect's name: Trevor Theys. But it was too late to check it out.

The next morning, the visit to the Criminal Records Centre across the road from the Cape Town Magistrates' Court was like hundreds Jonathan had made before. Going through the motions, he didn't have to wait long for the clerk to print out the familiar document. As always, he checked his notes to make sure the case number on the printout matched the one he had copied from the mugshot. Sea Point 44/09/1990. Use of a motor vehicle without the owner's consent.

Reading further, he saw that Theys had been found guilty and sentenced on 9 July 1991 to a fine of R500 or 100 days' imprisonment. He'd also earned a three-year suspended sentence of 200 days' imprisonment. That was it. The document in front of Jonathan showed that since 1991, Theys had not reoffended.

Just as I thought, Jonathan remembers telling himself. Theys is small fry.

As he turned to leave, a phrase in the document stopped him dead. The realisation was so great he had to sit down. Even now, recalling the moment, he says the hairs on the back of his neck and arms tingle. There it was in black and white. He had to read it again to make sure he was not seeing things. Since October 1995, Theys had been the legal owner of a CZ 7.65mm pistol. In that moment, Jonathan knew his luck had turned.

'Bliksem! I said to myself, Jonathan, do you realise that you are about to crack the biggest case of your career? My heart was in my throat. My hunger was back! This was my guy!'

Composing himself, Jonathan remained patient until nightfall, when he set out for the address on the printout: 48 Hector Road, Grassy Park. After a brief drive-by, he kept the house under surveillance for the next few days until he was sure Theys was not living there. When he eventually knocked, the woman who answered the front door had no forwarding address for Theys. But she knew where his wife lived in Grassy Park.

'Wie klop so hard aan my fokken deur?' yelled Janap Theys. *Who's banging so hard on my fucking door?* When she opened to Jonathan, he had his gun drawn and his backup team was surrounding her cottage.

She and Theys were no longer married, she explained. But Jonathan should find him living with his brother or sister in Sonderend Road in Portlands in Mitchells Plain.

Jonathan was struck by the irony of the address he wrote down. It was a mere kilometre from his own home!

'Meneer, don't trust them,' cautioned Janap. 'They can lie. If Trevor is not at his brother, you'll find him over the road at his sister. Catch him, Meneer, because he's not paying me maintenance.'

Then in her next breath she asked, 'Are you looking for Trevor for his speeding fines for my brother's white BMW?'

'Yes! That's exactly why we are here,' Jonathan replied.

He remembers smiling to himself as he and his team raced to Mitchells Plain.

'A white BMW... That's when I was sure that Theys was definitely my guy!'

While searching the brother's house, one of Jonathan's backup officers spotted someone peeping from behind a curtain across the road. The detective went over and knocked on the front door. A middle-aged man opened. The mugshot might have been old but it was without a doubt Mr Trevor Theys!

'It got better,' recalled Jonathan. 'After reading Theys his rights and cuffing him, his brother drew me aside. A month ago, he told me, he had laid a charge at Mitchells Plain when he discovered his pistol was stolen. He suspected Trevor was the culprit.'

What sort of pistol?

A Norinco 9mm.

Jonathan returned to Bishop Lavis with Theys and that familiar feeling of triumph.

'I attended the morning unit meeting and prepared my list of questions. By now I knew I was dealing with an amateur. One of the biggest massacres in Cape Town and both guns can be traced back to the shooters! Good heavens! My magtig!'

So you knew you could close the case?

'Oh yes! Definitely. I was *so* confident. I was ready. I was *so* ready. There was no way Theys was not going to work with me. Without me or anyone else laying a finger on him. Even if it took me the whole day.'

CHAPTER 7

CONFESSION

A nervous-looking Theys is sitting across the desk from Jonathan in a sixth-floor office commandeered for this long-cherished moment. It is one of the quietest in the Serious and Violent Crimes Unit's headquarters.

Jonathan wants the silence.

'I told Trevor Theys to relax. That this was not the end of the world. That we all make bad decisions in life.' Theys, a 43-year-old taxi driver who ferries sex workers to and from clients at night, doesn't reply. So Jonathan lets him ponder his words in silence while he pretends to page through his docket. It's a show. Jonathan knows the docket backwards. But he wants to surreptitiously watch Theys so he can read his body language. He wants to assess who he's up against.

Theys asks if he can smoke. Jonathan obliges, lighting up Theys's cigarette before dragging deeply on his own. Now the silence hangs in the smoke. Jonathan's good at this. During our interviews he'll sometimes remain so quiet on the phone I'll think he's hung up. And then when I inquire if he's still there, he'll reply, 'I'm listening'. Even though I'm not the one under interrogation, it's disquieting.

But today especially, Jonathan the Confessor Cop is in no hurry to say anything. Patience is the key. And the listening. That's where his power lies, not in the gun or the fist or the truncheon.

Suddenly, almost on cue, Theys blurts out a question: 'What evidence do you have against me?'

Jonathan smiles. Then he lists the white BMW getaway car, the pistol, the cartridges found at the scene, the stolen 9mm.

Theys says nothing. He looks scared. He can't hold eye contact and keeps shifting his eyes to the floor.

After weeks of disillusion and frustration, Jonathan can't believe it's going to be this easy. He dials down the tension by complimenting Theys on having aged gracefully since his mugshot. Theys asks for another cigarette and the two light up again. In the haze, Jonathan asks a few questions and has to suppress a smile when Theys tells him to relax. 'I just want to finish my smoke.'

Then Theys says, 'You've got the right person.'

'He sounded embarrassed,' recalls Jonathan.

What happens next is a bizarre first for Jonathan. 'This man who has murdered so brutally and callously asks if he can hug me.'

And as Jonathan lets him, Theys tells him: 'My life is in your hands.' Theys then cries and reveals he has a heart condition. Jonathan offers him his sandwich so his suspect can take his meds.

Then he listens without comment while Theys blames his partner in crime, 27-year-old restaurant manager Adam Woest, for his role in the Graham Road slaughter. 'I feared for my life because Adam said he wanted no loose ends. So I cut the victims softly.'

While Theys eats, Jonathan reflects. None of this would be happening right now if it weren't for Anna Louw. 'If she hadn't told De Villiers about the old albums and he hadn't said bring them, then Theys wouldn't be eating my sandwich in front of me. I was grateful to them both.'

Afterwards, Jonathan would thank Anna whenever he bumped into her at Sea Point Police Station. 'For the rest of my career I couldn't stop thanking her. That's the thing about being a detective. It's teamwork. There are so many people who helped me crack my cases and made me look like a hero. Without them I was nothing.'

Back to Theys. Once he had taken his meds, Jonathan knew he had to get him to a magistrate chop-chop or his confession was worth nothing in court. 'I was a warrant officer at that stage,' he reiterates. 'Only commissioned officers or magistrates can take a legally binding statement.'

By late afternoon, Theys's full confession is signed and sealed. He has also pointed out Woest's Bordeaux flat, which has a bird's eye view of Sizzlers from its walkway. Soon Jonathan joins his undercover colleagues watching Woest's workplace, Quay 4, at the V&A Waterfront. Identifying himself and asking the manageress for privacy, Jonathan spots Woest frying seafood in the kitchen as she guides him to her office. 'The manageress almost fell on her back when I told her why we were there.'

Back at Sea Point Police Station, Jonathan sits an anxious Woest down in the conference room. 'How do you know about me,' blurts out the mass murder who thought he had left no loose ends.

'Trevor spilt the beans,' says Jonathan, watching Woest's every twitch. 'You supplied the rope, the balaclavas, the surgical gloves and the petrol. Trevor supplied the guns and the white BMW.'

Woest is astonished. A total look of disbelief in his eyes. Then Jonathan brings it home: 'Trevor made a full confession to a magistrate implicating you as the mastermind. He told me everything.'

'Woest was shocked,' recalls Jonathan. 'I knew then we had him. Die koeël was deur die kerk.'

First Woest said it was Trevor's idea, then he asked to make a confession before a magistrate. By 10.30pm Jonathan had his second confession in the bag.

It had taken 23 days, Jonathan's longest wait ever.

Two days later the two men appeared in Cape Town Magistrates' Court on nine counts of murder and one of attempted murder.

CHAPTER 8

JUDGEMENT DAY

Despite the confessions, there is no motive for the massacre. Even in the High Court trial Woest and Theys didn't explain their extreme cruelty and violence as they declined to testify. Calling it 'one of the worst massacres Cape Town has experienced', Judge Nathan Erasmus, too, struggled to make sense of the incomprehensible in his March 2004 judgement.

'Shortly before midnight on 19 January 2003, accused number 1 (Woest) made a telephonic booking at Sizzlers. The plan was that both he and accused number 2 (Theys) would go there. Unbeknown to the occupants at No. 7 Graham Road, the two accused had no intention of utilising the services offered by Sizzlers but were fostering an evil and criminal intent.

'Around midnight they arrived at Sizzlers, after carefully plotting their plan. Accused number 2 had stolen his brother's firearm and obtained the use of a BMW motor vehicle. They armed themselves with two firearms, a knife, rope, duct tape, a two-litre container filled with petroleum, surgical gloves and balaclavas.

'They state that their primary goal for visiting Sizzlers was to rob the occupants. Upon their arrival the front door was opened by one of the deceased, Sergio De Castro, whereafter they were taken to a massage studio and Sergio returned to another massage studio to complete his services with a client, Berghaus. According to Quinton Taylor, the only eyewitness and sole survivor of the events, this was not normal procedure.

'On the night in question the sex workers did not get the

opportunity to present themselves to the accused. Shortly after the accused entered the premises, the owner, Eric Otgaar, appeared in the doorway of the dormitory with both the accused following. They were now wearing surgical gloves that they did not wear when entering the premises. Both were armed with firearms.

'The occupants of the house were told that it was a robbery. The two accused wore no disguises. Accused number 1 spoke to Eric as if they were known to each other. Eric was told to open the safe in the dormitory. Cash was found that the two accused shared. All those present in the dormitory were tied up by binding the hands and feet together. They were also forced to lie face down.

'Quinton insisted on lying on his back and was allowed to do so. He testified that he wanted to see if he got killed. This reminds one of the famous last words of Che Guevara when he told the person who shot him, before being shot, "I know you. You came to kill me. Shoot, coward, you are only going to kill the man."

'All of the occupants of the dormitory were gagged by having a sock stuck in their mouths and tied over with the duct tape. Their personal belongings, including jewellery and watches, were taken. According to Quinton Taylor, Eric and himself tried to hide their belongings but this was spotted by accused number 1, who was taking the lead, and ordered them to hand their belongings over.

'The two accused left the dormitory and went to the kitchen. When they returned accused number 1 was armed with a steak knife and accused number 2 had his own knife that he had earlier used to cut the rope with which the victims were tied up.

'At this stage Sergio and Berghaus (the client) were still in the adjacent room. Accused number 2 stayed with the people in the dormitory whilst accused number 1 was wandering through the house. Judging from the photographs and the objective evidence, he must have been looking for valuables or something that he could find.

'In Eric's room was a second safe that was also opened according to the evidence of his brother-in-law. According to Taylor, there was at least R7 000 in the safe that he brought from Knysna.

'The people in the dormitory asked accused number 2 if they were going to die, but were assured that it would not happen. However, shortly thereafter both accused started to cut their throats. The accused started from opposite ends and worked their way towards the centre. According to Taylor, accused 2 was hesitant to do it but was ordered to proceed by accused number 1.

'Whilst this was happening and shortly thereafter, the victims were screaming and moaning as a result of the cuts to their throats. Accused number 2 was constantly trying to calm accused number 1 and reassured the victims that they would not die.

'Later accused number 1 left the room and came back with the two litre container filled with petroleum and doused the victims. Thereafter, accused number 1 was walking up and down the house and it appeared as if he was talking to somebody on a cellphone. Taylor was under the impression that he was waiting for transport in order to leave.

'As time went on, the bonds loosened and accused number 2 re-tied them continuously. At one stage Eric Otgaar managed to get loose, but was knocked down by accused number 1. Later again accused number 1 left the room whilst number 2 stayed behind with the people in the dormitory.

'Shots were fired in another part of the house. This must have been when Sergio and Berghaus were shot. When accused number 1 returned to the room, both him and number 2 started shooting the people in the dormitory, again starting from left and right and working their way to the centre. It is common cause that all those present were shot, execution style.

'Taylor sustained serious injuries and survived miraculously. He ran to a nearby filling station and sought help. The two accused left the premises shortly after 3 o'clock. When leaving, they covered their faces with their balaclavas and ran to the get-away car that was parked nearby. The guns were later disposed of by accused number 2.'

'Mr Stephen, who appeared on behalf of the State, submitted that the accused went to Sizzlers to rob and had no intention to leave any survivors, meaning that not only was the robbery pre-meditated, but also that the idea to massacre was preconceived.

'Mr Calitz, on behalf of accused number 1, submitted that the killings were executed on the spur of the moment, after Berghaus was accidentally shot, following an attack on the accused by Berghaus.

'The possibilities stemming from the telephone conversations are legion, but to limit them to the complicity of others would be pure speculation. However, this raises certain questions that remain a mystery. In dealing with the contrary and opposing submissions made by Mr Calitz and Mr Stephen, the following factors, inter alia, are taken into account:

(a) Taylor's evidence of the whereabouts of the two accused at the time of the shooting of Berghaus is uncontested, therefore it would have been impossible for Berghaus to be shot in the circumstances as submitted by Mr Calitz.

(b) It must be accepted that accused number 1 was either known to Eric Otgaar, or the probabilities of being identified afterwards would have been good and he would have been aware of this. They took along balaclavas but never used them. Was this possibly because they knew there would be no survivors?

(c) They took along a two-litre container of petrol. Mr Calitz submits it was for the purposes of torture. Why? Why did they want to torture the people? To gain access to the money? If so, why use it after they had the money? Therefore, the purpose of the torture or the dousing of the individuals with the petroleum had nothing to do with robbery. The question arises why the torture, or is Mr Stephen correct in his submission that the only reasonable inference was that they wanted to obliterate the evidence.

(d) We know that they slit the victims' throats. Why? It could not have been with the intention to enforce submission to the robbery because at that time they had the money. Why then slit their throats? Was this to torture, as Mr Calitz has put it, or possibly to humiliate the victims, or did they have another motive?

(e) The robbery was completed shortly after their arrival on the scene. Why did they not leave then? The possibilities of complications must have crossed their minds. This scene was a 24-hour business venture, potential clients could arrive and in fact did arrive. Why the delay of almost three hours?

(f) Judging by the position of the shots, the number of shots fired at the victims, the accused had only one intention and that was to kill. The question arises why shoot to kill if you only came to rob?

(g) Even if the first shot that struck Berghaus was accidental, why proceed with the massacre?

I have no doubt that the submissions by Mr Calitz on the fact that the primary intention was robbery, is without merit. We are of the view that the only inference is that the two accused went to the scene with the premeditated intention to kill everyone they found, and robbery.'

The nine life sentences handed down by Judge Erasmus, Jonathan found fitting. But the many unanswered questions lingered.

'I couldn't find closure.'

Four months later he made the long drive to Caledon to Helderstroom Maximum.

Theys was happy to see Jonathan. Until he started pressing the mass murderer for answers.

'The smile on his face disappeared when I asked him why they tortured the boys. Why did they execute them. Why did you play "Tell It Like It Is" over and over? He kept blaming Woest. Telling me again and again that it was a robbery gone wrong.

I stopped our interview. It was clear that he didn't want to answer my difficult questions. I had a lonely trip home without the answers. And it still bothers me that I still don't have them.'

PART 2

KILLER COUNTRY

CHAPTER 9

THE HEAD IN THE BOX

May 2000 – April 2002

Once Jonathan had told me about Sizzlers, he selected other cases for his memoir. He did this often in the small hours of the night after his trauma nightmares woke him. Somehow the typing not only calmed him but spurred him on. This meant by the time we started collaborating again in late 2023, he was able to walk me through the mayhem and madness of his cop life. There was no need for Plan B, where I would compile those chapters from the police and court archives.

Jonathan's return to our project was also with brisk purpose. Whenever I dragged my heels or got side-tracked by my day job, he hustled me.

'Hi Mike,' he WhatsApps one day. 'I thought you forgot about me. I hope we can finalise this book asap. My family, friends and colleagues keep asking when the book will be finished and I have no answers. They are really excited. I'm getting old and hope to enjoy the book with my family and friends whilst still around.'

Now as we moved through his cases, Jonathan responded promptly whenever I 'advokaated' him. Metaphorically, we went from one high-profile case to the next in his red Toyota with 200 000km on the clock. Eventually, in 2004, Commissioner Mzwandile Petros replaced it with a new, royal-blue BMW 323i. And Jonathan was promoted to captain.

His laptop therapy also had a memory spin-off. He remembered dates at will without checking his files. And recalled details from decades ago as if it were yesterday. Jonathan was on a roll.

The next case he selected dated back to 17 May 2000.

The Morris clan were joking over a Wednesday night supper on that evening, when radio control called about a bizarre crime scene just five minutes away from his mother's Bulawayo Close home. One minute the detective inspector was laughing his head off. The next he was interviewing the complainant, a Mrs Blood, about a victim who had literally lost his head.

Mrs Blood was a nervous wreck. A box inside a black plastic crate had been dumped in her backyard by a tall stranger who fled into the night. When she opened the brown cardboard box, inside was a man's head, staring up at her. As word of her grisly find spread through a neighbourhood terrorised by the Mongrels gang, a crowd gathered on her doorstep. By the time Jonathan arrived, their demands to see the head had forced first responders to whisk the box to the safety of their Mitchells Plain Police Station.

The baying crowd had moved to the station by the time Jonathan got there at 8pm. He had to force his way through the mob to get inside, where a nervous constable pointed to the crate lying in the middle of the charge office. Jonathan braced himself but still recoiled as he gingerly removed a blue-and-yellow jacket covering the blood-soaked box inside the crate.

As was the case with Mrs Blood, this was the first time in his life, let alone his 23-year career, that he had been faced with a beheading. His first thought was, how was it possible that people could be so cruel? There should be no mercy for the perpetrators. There is no place for these animals in our community.

'I was sad and then filled with rage as I stared down at the head,' he told me. 'The deceased looked so peaceful. This man had just had his head chopped off, but he looked as if he was sleeping. It might sound bizarre, but the only thing out of place in that moment was a missing body.'

Jonathan's inner monologue was abruptly interrupted by arriving colleagues, including his unit commander, who asked him to lead the investigation, apologising for adding to the detective's case load. Jonathan already had 10 open gang-related murder dockets on his desk.

'I'll send these motherfuckers straight to jail where they belong,' he told his senior officer. Jonathan seldom swore but he was gatvol of the gangs, especially the 28s (a Numbers gang), who were the focus of two of his current cases. One of them involved the murder of a Valhalla Park doctor in his surgery. This had taken Jonathan to a 28s hideout, where he and colleagues liberated six teenage sex slaves kidnapped from an Athlone nightclub.

An hour later, after the head, box and crate had been photographed, Jonathan turned his attention to the crowd outside. He suspected among them would be someone who might recognise the head. Intuitively, he invited in six weather-beaten homeless women. These old aunties, he reckoned, would probably do a better job than the new-fangled CCTV facial recognition.

'O my fok, dis Donnie!' screamed one as Jonathan unveiled the crate. [It's Donnie.]

'How could they do this to Kaffertjie?' wailed another.

The man's name was Donovan de Jongh and he sold blades and pegs at Mitchells Plain Town Centre. The nickname was typical Cape Flats political incorrectness and referred to his dark complexion. Kaffertjie was everyone's friend, the mob exclaimed. The pig that had done this should be killed, was the crowd's consensus.

Jonathan appealed for witnesses and into the station walked Fatima Hendricks. She said that she had encountered a man called Curly on AZ Berman Drive at about 6pm. He asked her if she wanted a sheep's head and feet. You cannot make this up, mused Jonathan. Curly was with a tall stranger carrying a black plastic crate.

About 15 minutes later, Fatima noticed a crowd gathering at the traffic lights and there she found Curly lying injured on the tar. She heard that gangsters had beaten him up when they discovered the head in the crate was not a sheep's head.

Now Donnie's parents arrived in the charge office and his

mother promptly fainted as she identified her adopted 28-year-old, law-abiding son who was intellectually disabled.

'He did not deserve to die this way,' she sobbed, as she slowly recovered, tears streaming down her face.

'I was shocked when I saw the head for the first time,' says Jonathan. 'Then I got busy and pushed my feelings aside. But the mother's tears threw me.'

Not for long. Jonathan blocked his emotions with a practised effortlessness before they could turn to tears. 'I had to focus. There was still a lot of investigation ahead.'

A clue dropped into place when the detective learnt that first responders had earlier arrested the bleeding Curly as soon as members of the Junior Cisko Yakkies gang explained the situation. One of Curly's assailants was the son and bodyguard of notorious Yakkies drug dealer, Brian Khan. Curly and another tall man had arrived at his father's shebeen with a delivery, he told cops.

In a scene fit for *The Godfather*, bodyguards peered down at the head in the box. For a moment they could hardly believe the audacity of the unspeakable threat before them. Then out came broomsticks and they beat the two men all the way down to AZ Berman Drive until Curly collapsed. His accomplice managed to escape.

'I still chuckle at the image of this long guy running for his life, but not letting go of that crate,' says Jonathan. 'He must have been so panic-stricken that he forgot he was carrying the head until he got to Mrs Blood's house.'

Late that first night, Jonathan called on Mr Khan for a heart-to-heart. By now his network would probably know the name of Curly's accomplice. He found Khan kakking himself. Seriously anxious. The threat was implicit: his head was next.

'Relax, Mr Khan,' said Jonathan. 'Think long and hard about who's the best person to help you keep your head'.

'He didn't reply', Jonathan recalls, 'but Khan's expression told me all I needed to know. Later that night he promised that his bodyguards would make statements.'

Before knocking off, Jonathan popped into Mitchells Plain Day Hospital at 2am for a word with Curly, now identified as Melvin Muggels.

'I had some serious questions. But his police guard told me he was still in a Zulu blues. Don't ask me why, but that's police slang for dronk. Truly drunk.'

Jonathan got little sleep that night and early the next morning was on his way to interview Muggels when radio control turned him around. Instead of passing the tip-off on to him, the excitable Mitchells Plain mobile squad had broken the chain of command. Too often Jonathan had seen investigations compromised by such rash behaviour. But thankfully this time it seemed like only good news.

Their early morning knock found Mrs Muggels, who pointed them to her son's boss across the road. The tall Roger Jones immediately showed them his pair of bloodied jeans, and revealed the name of a third accomplice, Anwar Abrahams. He also told them they could find poor Donnie's headless corpse in the bush opposite the Lentegeur Psychiatric Hospital.

'I found the deceased lying on his back covered with a white refuse bag,' recalls Jonathan with still palpable distress. 'His hands were clenched in fists. I knew right then that Donnie must have suffered. But I never imagined how cruel his suffering was.'

By midday, Jonathan had the crime scene wrapped and his suspect's blood, hair and DNA samples in the lab. He was certain they'd find crime scene matches that would put the two away. And, less than 24 hours into his investigation, Roger Jones was confessing how he, Muggels and Abrahams picked up Donnie at the town centre and drove to the crime scene to eat a Gatsby (a sandwich filled with chips and meat). Jones explained he was drunk from drinking most of the day and decided to sleep in his car when Abrahams, Muggels and the deceased Donnie went to smoke a dagga-and-Mandrax pipe in the bush. They returned with Donnie's crate, which they loaded into the boot.

'Where was Donnie?' Jonathan asked, noting the 28s gang tattoo on Jones's upper right arm. There were no epaulettes on his shoulders, telling Jonathan that Jones was merely a low-ranking soldier.

'It was not my business to ask questions,' replied a jittery Jones, continually shifting in his chair. 'I was still half-drunk and wanted to get home. Go ask Anwar and Melvin about that.'

It didn't matter to the detective that Jones was distancing himself from the beheading. In 30 minutes, he had placed all three actors at the crime scene. And Jones conceded that Donnie's blood rubbed off on his jeans as he loaded the crate. That was enough for now.

'It was by no means an easy interview,' Jonathan confessed. 'Jones was hardegat and couldn't look me in the eye.'

But Jonathan remained deadpan, as hard as that was when Jones denied running away from the shebeen pursued by a swarm of angry broomsticks.

'Inside,' says Jonathan, 'I was laughing my head off at the mental movie of this giraffe and his crate. You can imagine, né? Remember I'm the pastor. I don't fight with the sinners. I make them comfortable so that they open up and repent. I forgive them, because they know not what they do.'

Less than 48 hours into Jonathan's investigation, Muggels was sober enough to talk. But he was petrified. He had witnessed Donnie's horrific decapitation by Abrahams but dared not go on record for fear of losing his own head.

Jonathan wasn't too bothered by this.

'I didn't want to push Muggels too hard. I had to give him space and respect his decision not to make a statement. I also knew in my heart that if I was patient, I'd get my chance to swing him.'

Next up, a few hours later, came Abrahams. He and Jones were old chommies in crime. Both had served seven years for a gangland murder where Jones had done the stabbing.

From the get-go Abrahams, also a 28s, was windgat and in denial. Instead of answering questions, he fired off his own around Curly's version of events. Normally Jonathan would have let his fishing expedition go. But it was too soon after Donnie's distressing post-mortem six hours earlier. Blood analysis showed Donnie drank about four drinks before he realised he was being set up. But that wasn't nearly enough alcohol to unclench his fists as he was killed. For the first time in more than 40 murder suspect interviews, Jonathan got angry.

'You are a useless piece of shit coward. You are a bully who slaughtered a soft target who could not defend himself. You haven't got the balls to try this with another gangster. I hope you rot in hell.'

Ending the interview without another word, Jonathan instructed a colleague: 'Take this coward's fingerprints before I break his fingers.' Then he drove to his mother's home to watch a movie to calm down.

A week later the detective got another vital piece of evidence when he visited Jones's girlfriend. She confided that he was tired of having no money. 'Jones told her he was going to sort his cash flow by executing a drug dealer to get respect from other merchants, who would then be intimidated into paying him protection money.'

The girlfriend thought it was a joke. Until Jonathan shocked her by telling her how her boyfriend and his buddy had lured Donnie into a trap. She refused to make a statement. Her story affirmed the detective's instinct about Khan. He must have heard this story through the gangland grapevine. Even with Jones and Abrahams behind bars, Khan never went anywhere, including to court, without bodyguards.

Better still, the girlfriend's confession inspired Jonathan. They were the worst kind of bullies. They could not have picked a softer target than Donnie. And if there's one thing Jonathan still can't handle it's a bully. Right then and there he vowed Jones, and Abrahams in particular, would pay. No matter how long or what it took.

Many weeks later, the fingerprint analysis report emerged from the lab bottleneck. It put Muggels, Abrahams and Jones in the latter's car that had been parked at the crime scene. But Jonathan's spirits were dashed when delayed DNA results landed on his desk. They could only link Muggels and Jones to Donnie.

He cursed the eager-beaver Mitchells Plain officers. When they arrested Abrahams, they had neglected to search his house for his bloodied clothes. That meant Jonathan only had Donnie's blood on Jones's jeans. This mistake might prove costly come the trial.

What bugged the detective more was that he only had partial confessions. A full confession that would put this investigation to bed still eluded him.

For 18 months, Jonathan accepted that Abrahams would eventually walk. And then he found serenity when a new prosecutor preparing Donnie's murder case for trial in the High Court called him in early February 2002. Her predecessor had dropped all charges against Abrahams and he had been released. But she was keen to pursue the possibility of applying new plea bargain legislation to this case. Designed to speed up trials, the legislation empowered state prosecutors to cut a sentencing deal with an accused who was willing to shop his co-conspirators with damning evidence.

Jonathan took Advocate Annette de Lange at her word and launched the undercover operation he'd been hatching ever since Abrahams gave him the finger. An operation he was sure would yield the confession he craved. But he had to move with cunning and stealth. Abrahams was out of the way, but Jones was still in Pollsmoor, a 28s stronghold infested with impimpis [betrayers], even among the warders.

Sometime back a Mitchells Plain cop transporting awaiting-trial prisoners to and from court had given him the contact details of a Pollsmoor deputy head who could be trusted. All it took was one call.

'Leave it with me,' said the official after listening to Jonathan's plan. 'I know what to do.'

The detective can't remember the exact date, but he arrived at Pollsmoor on a bright Wednesday at around 10am. Except, instead of reporting to reception as he usually did, he followed the deputy's directions to an unfamiliar heavy steel gate away from prying eyes. It led to a small office, where he checked in his Vektor Z88 9mm, then an officer silently led him to a private office off limits to offenders. As if it was yesterday, Jonathan recalls the smell of floor polish as he entered the room. And the startled look of the offender, who sat obediently behind the desk. He hadn't been told why he was there. And the last person he was expecting was detective Jonathan Morris.

The steady hum of the air-conditioner and a phone ringing in another office broke the silence as the detective sat down. For a long time he had known this kid was the master key. From the first time he saw this 19-year-old in court he noticed the fear in his eyes. And his abandoned expression as he scoured the back of the court for support that was never there. The scene was so familiar to the detective.

'I felt sorry for him every time I saw him. He was a lost boy.'

Jonathan dug deeper and learnt Muggels' grandmother had raised him in Elsies River from the age of three, when his mother left to live with her new boyfriend in Stellenbosch. He had never met his father. What surprised Jonathan when he read the kid's profile in 2000 was that he hadn't been groomed by a gang. He was certainly ripe for it after being expelled in primary school for fighting and regular truancy. But his only brushes with the law were for petty theft. Then he made a bad decision that threatened to wreck his life for good. Unless he opened to the redemption sitting in front of him.

Jonathan sensed this had sunk in by the time he broke the silence with a greeting. Then he listened as the youngster lamented that Jonathan was his first and only visitor since his June 2000 arrival at Pollsmoor. For a moment it broke Jonathan's heart. But he couldn't afford sentiment to interfere with swinging this offender. He laid out his case kindly but firmly.

'Donnie's blood and DNA were found on your clothes. I have witnesses saying you had his head at the shebeen. I've got enough for the judge to put you away for life.'

The kid started crying, recalls Jonathan, who then made his play.

'Do you know the case against Anwar has been dropped?'

He looked shocked.

'Do you know why?'

Silence.

'He has turned state witness and will tell the court that you lured Donnie into the car and then later cut off his head.'

A quick flash of understanding in the eyes of the now 21-year-old told Jonathan that Muggels realised he too had been set up by Jones and Anwar. They were his bullies as well.

'Hy lieg, meneer, he lies,' exclaimed Muggels, almost falling from his chair. 'Dis hy wat Donnie se kop afgesaag het! Dis hy!' [He cut off Donnie's head. It's him.]

Jonathan was about to add that Jones, too, would swear Muggels was the beheader. But it wasn't necessary because there is no stopping the truth when it will out. The detective compiled the shocking confession. Then he instructed Muggels to keep their meeting a secret.

'Just tell your lawyer exactly what you told me. Tell him the truth and show remorse and he will look after you. He'll get you a lesser sentence. If you don't do this, you will spend the rest of your life in prison.'

Jonathan was bending the rules meeting Muggels without his lawyer. Handing him a R20 note and pack of cigarettes on his way out could be construed as an inducement. If Muggels got cold feet, it could all blow up in his face, adversely affecting the case and his reputation. But sometimes justice gets messy.

The detective was whistling Bob Marley's 'Three Little Birds' when he reached his red Corolla. The lyrics, 'Don't worry about a thing, cause every little thing is gonna be alright' lingered all the way to Kalk Bay Fisheries, where he celebrated the confession he'd heard over a hake-and-chips parcel in a sunny ocean breeze. Then he took a slow drive to town to deliver the confession to De Lange, no questions asked.

'I was at peace,' recalls Jonathan. 'My canary had sung and very soon I knew that I would have my other two birds back together in the cage where they belonged.'

Come the last day in February, De Lange called with good news.

The confession was now a formal plea bargain. And she had a warrant for Abrahams' arrest.

'I dropped everything and raced to her office,' recalls Jonathan. 'We shook hands but I was so excited I flung my arms around her.'

He later found Abrahams drinking beer at a friend's house in Rocklands. 'When he asked if he could finish his beer before being cuffed, I laughed in his face and crossed my fingers that he'd resist. I was itching to give the bastard a hiding.'

Jonathan could not wait for 18 March 2002, when his three birds entered the dock. Abrahams and Jones thought they were appearing to make sure all the ducks were in a row for their High Court trial. Until, that is, Muggels' lawyer handed up the first plea bargain in South African legal history. The detective watched as they silently turned to look at each other's stricken faces.

'I could almost see the penny drop as the lawyer began reading it to Judge Desai,' remembers Jonathan with delight. 'The writing was on the wall.'

The court heard that Muggels, Abrahams and Jones spent the morning getting drunk and smoking Mandrax before driving to the town centre. While Muggels waited in the car, Abrahams and Jones went to buy food. The pair returned to the car with Donnie. They then drove to the bush opposite Lentegeur.

While Jones remained in the car, the trio walked a short way into the bush. One moment Donnie was smoking a dagga-and-Mandrax pipe with them, the next Abrahams was stabbing him in the neck. 'Donnie grabbed his neck and Anwar Abrahams kicked him away from us. I (Melvin Muggels) got up and ran to the car and told Roger Jones what just happened. Roger did not say anything, as if he knew it was going to happen. Anwar came to the car and told Roger to drive to his friend in Tafelsig, where they fetched a saw. Anwar said that he was going to saw Donnie's head off and it must be delivered to Brian Khan, a well-known drug dealer. We went back to the bush. After Anwar beheaded Donnie, he placed the head in the plastic crate and loaded it in the boot.'

Back at Jones's home, the trio smoked more dagga and Mandrax before Abrahams ordered that Donnie's head be delivered to Khan.

Muggels' co-accused were livid by the time Desai sentenced him to the agreed 15 years instead of life.

As he made his way down to the cells, protected by a police orderly and Jonathan, Abrahams yelled, 'Melvin, what the fuck have you done? Where does this come from?'

Gone was the fear in Muggels's face. Remaining silent, he just grinned at Abrahams and Jones as if to say, fuck you.

Jonathan drove Muggels to Victor Verster Correctional Centre to begin his sentence out of the reach of his co-accused. 'I kept him sweet by driving his aunt and his mother to visit him every week,' explains Jonathan. 'His mother had come back into his life in his early teens. She wanted to visit him in Pollsmoor but never had the money for transport from Tafelsig.'

Muggels returned the favour a month later in the High Court, this time as the state's star witness. His excellent testimony put Abrahams and Jones away for life for murder, kidnapping and intimidation.

With a happy wave to his family and Donnie's parents sitting alongside them in the gallery, followed by a smiling doff of the head to his father confessor, Muggels was gone. His courageous plea bargain was more than a legal death knell to a pair of conniving murderers. More than one detective's crusade.

Muggels's truth set him free, ending his endless nightmares about headless Donnie, once a familiar face who lived two streets away from the Tafelsig home he shared with his mother, Cornelia. It was also Muggels's way of saying sorry. Not only to his mother but also to Donnie's grieving parents.

A court can only accept a plea bargain with the legal blessing of the victim's family and the investigating officer. Recognising Melvin's olive branch, Shariefa and Moegamat Jacobs signed, grateful for the truth that brought them peace and closure. Their blessing also opened a door to reconciliation with Cornelia. Their common ground was that they were all grieving lost boys. In time they healed enough to travel to the trial together in the back of Jonathan's Toyota Corolla.

The detective never saw them or his three birds again. As was the case for Melvin Muggels, Jonathan's recurrent nightmares of Donnie's poor head in the box receded. And that was that.

Until a few weeks later, when the case came to him in his sleep one last time. Head back on his shoulders, Donnie was happily selling blades in the town centre on a mild spring day. Looking the detective dead in the eye, he smiled while whistling a familiar tune. It was already fading by the time the Confessor Cop woke. But to this day he swears it was 'Three Little Birds'.

CHAPTER 10

REIGN OF TERROR

July 2001 – May 2004

My only comfort is Detective Sergeant Chauke next to me, behind the wheel of my Red Toyota. We've been around the block long enough to know we've got each other's backs. But it's cold comfort. It's early morning, mid-July on the freezing, deserted streets of Gugulethu. The heater is turned up high. To keep us warm and to make sure my shooting hand is thawed. Because we're patrolling on the off chance we spot Wox and Nana. Because if we do then I will have to draw first. Otherwise these bastards will kill us like the half dozen before us.

Suddenly a white Polo pulls out ahead from a side road. The street lights are yellow-dim. But our headlights flash across the car's windows just enough for us to match instantly the mugshot that's been stuck to the dash for too many weeks.

The scene unfolds quickly but feels like slow motion. Chauke hits the gas. Not too much. Just enough to draw level with the Polo's back window. Any further, we've had it drilled into us, and they shoot you dead. Next thing Chauke is skilfully forcing the Polo off the road. He caresses the brakes to make sure we stay behind them as both cars draw to a standstill. Overshoot them and we can't use our open doors as cover.

My right hand is hungry for my Vektor lying warm and ready, safety off, on my lap. In one fluid motion, I cock it and reach for my door catch. The whole time I'm observing myself as if I'm not in my body. It feels like I'm directing a movie scene. The shit is about to hit the fan but I'm cool as a cucumber. I'm so ready to end this reign of terror.

Then things start to go so horribly wrong that I want to throw up.

In the motion of opening my door and cocking a round into the chamber, with 15 more to follow, my whole pistol falls apart. Parts scatter across the footwell and onto the ground outside. Frantically I try to scoop them up but my arms feel like jelly. Gunfire so close that it deafens me. The windscreen shatters and bullets thump into my seat. I should be hit but I'm not. It seems to take forever but eventually slippery hands reassemble my weapon and I'm pulling the trigger as Wox and Nana bear down on my Toyota. Thank God they're reloading, giving me a clear shot to end this without a long fucking trial.

But I watch in slow motion horror as a round emerges from my barrel, then dribbles to the ground. I squeeze the trigger again. Same thing. Again and again and again. Then their muzzles are blazing. Over and over again.

My whole world is deurmekaar [complete chaos]. I'm soaking wet. But when I reach out to touch my blood, there's no stickiness. Just sweat-soaked pyjamas and sheets. I reach for the beach towel I've been keeping next to my bed to wipe my face so that I can slip back into sleep. If I have to get up now, I'll be lying wide awake until sunrise.

Detective Inspector Jonathan Morris gazed down at the two bodies lying next to each other in the Nyanga East field. Even without forensics he knew they'd been told to lie face down in the cold, damp, winter dirt before being shot execution style in the back of the head. Which was odd, he thought, wondering if these petrified men knew what was coming as they dropped to their knees obediently. They were well dressed, civilians probably going about their business, not gangsters with a beef.

It was Jonathan's 42nd birthday. After reporting for standby duty two hours earlier at 7.30am sharp on 21 July 2001, his shift leader had given him the rest of the day off. Then called him while

75

he was en route to his mother's Mitchells Plain home. He was headed there for a celebratory lunchtime braai with his siblings and children.

'No, Colonel, I don't mind popping in at the crime scene. Moenie worry nie. [Don't worry.] I'm right here on Lansdowne Road. At Brown's Farm. It's only a few blocks away, Colonel.' Not far from this place of bittersweet childhood memories, buried below the teeming shacks that now hide what he once knew as Clear Water Farm.

Jonathan turned from the bodies and walked towards the noisy crowd behind the yellow police cordon, mulling over the pair of 7.65mm bullet casings the team had recovered along with a bullet point that had gone clean through one victim's head. The executioners didn't give a toss about their evidentiary trail. Or worse, they were so cocky they thought they were untouchable.

The crowd also put him on edge. The fear in their angry faces wasn't just about the bodies behind him, he thought. Then again, it could be the unfamiliarity of his first murder scene in a black township.

People here heard gunshots every night and lived in fear of faceless killers. Or so they told him when he turned his attention to the uniformed Nyanga cops who were first on the scene. They spoke of two hijackings in June, one of them involving a similar double execution. Rumours whispered the name Wox as the triggerman. Hadn't the detective heard, the cops asked, because the cases were with his Serious Crimes Unit. That was odd, thought Jonathan, certain he was up to speed with every murder his colleagues were investigating.

By the time Jonathan wrapped the scene at 12.30pm, his birthday braai had been cancelled and he was flooring his Toyota away from the peculiarities of the crime scene towards Nyanga Police Station to sign for the docket. The trail was still warm. The quicker he shut this case the sooner he could get back to the eight incomplete murder dockets on his desk.

Delft SAPS kept the detective moving forward. Earlier they had arrested a chop-shop owner in possession of a hijacked VW Golf. Family at the car's registered address provided descriptions of the hijack victims that matched the dead faces in his docket.

Chop-shop owner Mabulwana Baloyi was putty in the detective's hands the following morning. He snitched. Told him his regular clients, Nana and Wox from Gugulethu, had earlier delivered the Golf for stripping. And a few days before that, while stripping a Ford Midge for them, he'd noticed blood on the rear floor mats.

Jonathan left the interview with descriptions of the killers. Softly spoken Nana was short, well-built and about 18 years old. Wox was the one to watch out for. In his late twenties or early thirties, he was always high, said Baloyi. And aggressive.

At Monday's parade, Jonathan confirmed that his colleagues were indeed investigating at least three murders in and around Nyanga involving execution-style shots to the back of the head from a 7.65mm pistol. The name Wox was unfamiliar to them, but Jonathan's gut feel was that there was a link to his case.

Convinced, his commander appointed him lead investigator. The strategy was his colleagues should complete their investigations, leaving Jonathan to hunt down Wox and Nana. To investigate all the cases simultaneously would spell burnout.

Later that same day, while Baloyi was appearing in Bellville Magistrates' Court on stolen property charges, Jonathan's commander called. Another hijacking and double murder the previous night. This time a taxi driver and his passenger. They raped the woman before executing her and the driver in an abandoned Nyanga shack. The weapon? A 7.65mm.

What the hell is happening, thought Jonathan, bundling the remanded Baloyi into his Toyota. The chop-shop owner's vague suggestion in court that Wox was a Gugulethu resident was worth a look. Hell, it was the only damn lead he had right now.

Within the hour, there the bastard was in a Gugulethu detective's mugshot file. One Mthuthuzeli Nombewu. To this day Jonathan remembers his cold dark eyes. He looked like bad news.

But the detective was up for it. Wox's last known address was less than 10 minutes away.

Please let him be home, Jonathan prayed, pistol cocked as he hammered on the door with 10 Gugulethu detectives and uniformed cops tight as a laager around the red facebrick semi.

Mthuthuzeli had left more than three months ago, stammered his startled mother. For who knows where? 'Good riddance, because he stole everything I own for drug money.'

Deflated, the detective's next opportunity of getting Nombewu was at his scheduled appearance in four days at an Athlone court on TV theft charges. Rather than wait until then, he and Chauke drove around Gugulethu and Nyanga with Baloyi, hoping for an off-chance sighting. They were also hoping for a response from a township patrol van to their all-points bulletin.

Two days later, Wox and Nana showed the detective who was calling the shots. Another couple were hijacked and driven to an abandoned building near Crossroads. They were forced to lie face down in the dirt and shot. Miraculously they survived. The male, thinking his companion was dead, had crawled away to safety. She was found alive but blinded by the shooting. She died a year later.

'That coward wouldn't even talk to me,' Jonathan told me with disgust. 'He didn't want his wife to find out about his affair with the woman who died.'

By now it was clear Wox and Nana were a law unto themselves. It was unlikely Wox would appear in Athlone court that Friday. But he was also unpredictable. So Chauke carried out surveillance at court with backup firepower while Jonathan watched the post-mortems of the two young men, Siseko Nxu and Nceba Faltein, who had been found on his birthday.

As is often the case with serial murders, the killings stopped, typically escalating community anxiety and paranoia. The detective felt it too. The pause in the body count kept everyone guessing. Had the killers grown bored? Had they moved on or been arrested for a petty crime? Or, please God, had they been hit by a bus?

That's when Jonathan remembers his nightmares starting.

Always the same theme. Helplessness. Escalating to at least one every night. It didn't matter that Wox and Nana's guns were silent. In fact, the anticipation intensified his nightmares. As did the outside pressure.

By that stage Gugulethu Police Station was already a presidential priority station because of the high murder rate in the precinct. The community put pressure on the provincial commissioner and it ramped up along the chain of command until it landed with Inspector Morris. The top brass wanted answers Jonathan didn't have. He felt motive might provide a slender lead. But the only answers came via his vivid imagination.

The detective coped by following up every tip from the community. And by going to bed as late as he could in the vain hope it would stave off the nightmares.

'I was exhausted. When I did fall asleep it was only for two hours. Then I would jerk awake after a nightmare with the thought that they had struck again.'

For 13 anxious days Wox and Nana were silent. By then the detective's mind, not for the first time in his career, began playing a cruel trick. Even though experience told him otherwise, hope that the killers would not kill again turned into belief.

He began to breathe more easily. Sleep a little longer. Then, on day 19 of his investigation, Wox and Nana came back into play. On 8 August they hijacked a couple in Nyanga. They stopped to execute the man. And then later his partner, after they'd both raped her. Again 7.65mms were used. Muzzle-against-the-head style. Face down in the dirt.

Six hours later, in the early hours of 9 August, they put a bullet into the head of another woman, this time after masquerading as policemen to gain entry to her home. Then on Friday, 10 August, Jonathan's colleagues delivered their completed investigation dockets. Five in total. All linked by a familiar modus operandi and 7.65mm shells.

Now, flipping through crime scene photos and autopsy reports, Jonathan realised he was possibly dealing with one of the biggest serial killing cases since the Wemmer Pan Killer, Cedric Maake, had raped and murdered more than 27 women in the late-1990s.

Already the body count was 10. And it was only a matter of time before Wox and Nana would kill again.

The weekend was quiet. But the detective's mind circled from one case to the next. 'I searched the dockets for a clue I might have missed. That's when I started questioning my ability to solve this case,' recalls Jonathan. 'Chauke had one of the best informer networks of all township cops. The community was on high alert. Wox's mugshot was everywhere. They were leaving evidence all over the place. But we didn't have a solid lead. It was like Wox and Nana were ghosts. It was unnerving.'

They emerged from the shadows again that Sunday. At about 7pm on 12 August, a couple were executed in a Nyanga field. Same calibre pistol. Same modus operandi. The case was waiting for Jonathan at Monday morning's parade, where he could feel the awkwardness in the room. 'It was difficult looking my colleagues in the eye.'

He began visiting the crime scenes that he knew only from the new dockets on his desk. After each inspection, he and Chauke interviewed the victims' families. Chauke translating from Xhosa gave the detective a keener ear for possible clues. But there were none. Just consolation from families grateful that the detectives had taken the time to bring them up to speed. 'Their gratitude kept us moving forward but I gave myself a hard time for not giving them closure. The families needed a breakthrough as much as I did.'

As they went from one family to the next, the detectives had plenty of time to reflect on their nemeses. Clearly Wox and Nana had no impulse control. How much that had to do with personality or drugs was an unknown. A dead certainty was they had no fear of the police. In an accidental contact situation that would make the pair extremely dangerous.

While the detectives carried out their case-by-case due diligence, they were ever aware that Wox and Nana were hibernating yet again. 'The tension in the background was unbearable. It messed with my mind. It was like the bastards were playing with us. And I took it personally.'

More so when Wox and Nana struck on 20 August, again around 7pm just as Jonathan was knocking off. Again the killers hijacked a couple. Forced them to lie on the floor in the back of their VW Caravelle after robbing them. Wox and Nana then drove to their next killing field. Along the way they were distracted by two men firing warning shots as they pursued a group of youngsters who had been stoning their car.

Greedy for their guns, Wox played good Samaritan, offering the men a lift to speed up their chase. Timothy Ndabeni and Sydney Molefe accepted but quickly grew uneasy along the way, asking Vox to drop them back at their car. As Ndabeni and Molefe alighted, they were shot from behind. Unbeknown to Wox and Nana, they had just executed a police informer and seriously wounded his undercover handler, Sergeant Ndabeni. Ndabeni had been decorated for bravery a few months earlier. Wox and Nana put him in a wheelchair for the rest of his life.

Fleeing the scene, Wox collided with a parked bakkie. Pumping bullets into the back of the bakkie as they fled, the two men killed one of their victims, Vuyo Tati. Miraculously Tati's girlfriend, Nokonwaba May, escaped injury.

The body count now stood at 14 and Wox and Nana had also shot a cop. Again they disappeared into the shadows.

Jonathan recalls being irritated when Gugulethu Police Station called at 3pm on Saturday, 25 August, five days after Ndabeni had been shot. Part of the reason was the fact that Wox and Nana had fallen silent again. In truth he was irritated with himself. But it was easier to project the blame onto Gugulethu cops for the stagnancy of his investigation. Baloyi had picked out Wox's mugshot five weeks ago! But not one Gugulethu cop or informer knew him. Not one had spotted him on the street. It didn't add up. Why the hell couldn't they do their job?

Drop it, he told the complaining voice in his head as the officer explained how a routine patrol spotted four men fleeing from a hijacked Mazda 323 at about 6.30 that Saturday morning. They had caught one just after he dumped two 9mm pistols in a yard. He told them that Wox was one of the men who had escaped. Jonathan held his breath. The youngster's name was Asanda Baninzi, said the officer. But he goes by the nickname Nana!

Relief coursed through the detective. It had taken 36 days since his birthday but finally the breakthrough he'd prayed for had arrived. Maybe tonight the nightmares would stop.

Still drugged and boozed to the gills, Baninzi was in no state to be questioned when the detective arrived in his cell. He seemed confused. And afraid of the noisy lynch mob outside chanting for his blood.

Maybe, Jonathan reckoned, he could use this kid's fear if he dared apply for bail. Then, in a moment of bittersweet irony, Baninzi confessed he was haunted by all the dead bodies that would not let him sleep. 'As soon as he said that, I knew I had him. Give me a few hours tops with this boy, and I'll have him singing like a canary.'

The detective's initial bullishness was tempered on the Sunday morning when he visited Baninzi's mother. It was a calculated move. He needed to know what pressed his suspect's buttons. But his visit wasn't without compassion. If the roles were reversed, he would want to be told, first hand, that he had spawned a monster.

Not for the first time in his career, the detective was struck by the dissonance of visits like these. His most-wanted serial killer lived in an utterly average semi-detached with a neat flower bed out front. And here was his concerned mother sitting before him on her fading floral couch, worried sick about her mild-mannered boy.

'That's when it sunk in,' recalls Jonathan. 'My suspect was a schoolboy!'

As expected, Mrs Baninzi didn't cope well with the detective's awful news. She knew something was amiss with her 18-year-old that she had raised alone since his father walked out on them when the boy was just nine. He'd dropped out of high school in June and she'd argued with him to get him to return. He wouldn't. Instead her TV and other valuables started disappearing. She worried about the whiff of dagga in his room. And by his prolonged disappearance from home in July.

But how, appealed Mrs Baninzi in between deep sobs, how, sir, is it possible her Asanda could kill so many?

Her bewilderment triggered the Confessor Cop. He hugged her with tears in his eyes, whispering, 'don't worry, Mama. I will treat your son well.'

'What happened back there?' asked a concerned Chauke as they drove to collect Baninzi for questioning.

'No mother should go through such pain,' replied Jonathan, pulling his hard-arsed detective self together. 'Especially when she tried her best as a single mom.'

Back at headquarters, Baninzi was grateful to Jonathan for giving him a bar of soap and the neatly ironed set of clothes he had got his mother to pack. While he freshened up in the bathroom, Jonathan laid out his 10 dockets in the office used for the morning briefings. On a Sunday morning, without a soul around, the fourth-floor office seemed to intimidate suspects. Jonathan had noticed long ago that they would keep glancing at the empty chairs around the table, almost as if expecting the bad cop to show up. He juxtaposed that tension with his regulation pre-interview steak-and-kidney pie and Coke that was waiting for the spruced-up boy. He could see the delight in Baninzi as he approached his seat, trembling not just from hunger but also creeping Mandrax withdrawal.

Breakfast wolfed down, Jonathan maintained a deliberate silence, the only sound being the strong southeaster slapping against the windows. He let it get uncomfortable before announcing that he had spared Baninzi having to break his unspeakable behaviour to his mother. The kid's relief was visible. Then he spoke to the boy about his lost father bringing tears to his eyes.

Jonathan can't clearly recall his next words but they went something like: 'Your mother trusts me to look after you. So I think it would be in your best interest to trust me as well, because she and I know you are not capable of killing so many people on your own.'

Even after all these years of interviewing, the Confessor Cop was taken aback by how effortlessly a suspect would 'sing'. This time it was the song that nearly knocked him from his chair. Part of the lyrics mentioned one Shadrack.

Who was Shadrack?

What had happened was that, after his arrest, the Gugulethu cops got Baninzi to reveal Wox's hideout. By the time they kicked down the Nyanga shack door, he was gone. But they found lots of the loot listed in their dockets, as well as the names of the two men who had escaped with Wox: Shadrack Nontshongwana and Thembekile Malusi.

In Baninzi's confession, the problem was the mother. She ran the spaza shop opposite their Delft hideout in the backyard of Wox's sangoma aunt. She threatened to call the cops because she knew the boys were chopping stolen cars in the bush nearby. That's why the Gugulethu cops couldn't find these bastards, thought the detective, steeling himself for the details.

At first Baninzi and Wox laughed off Felicity Adams, the spaza shop owner. But while smoking Mandrax in a drug house down the road, they saw the cops raid their hideout. That signed her death warrant. Because Wox was pissed off he had no place to sleep that night.

Jonathan sat dead still watching Baninzi, who evaded eye contact. For a man who thought he'd seen it all, heard it all, listening to this kid justifying without a twitch of remorse the revenge slaughter of not just a mother, but her husband and their two children, was beyond belief.

Baninzi confirmed one of the 9mm pistols he had dumped while fleeing the Gugulethu cops had been used in the slaying. When Jonathan tried to establish who pulled the trigger, he noticed how easily the boy blamed Shadrack. And that as he did so he slid down in his chair, almost as if he was slipping away from culpability.

At that point the detective wanted to bark, sit up! The boy was taking advantage of his kindness. But he let it slide. All he had to do was allow Baninzi to blame away and he'd still have him for all the dockets on the table.

Shadrack was returning a favour by killing the lady, explained the boy. It was his way of thanking Wox for sharing his dagga and Mandrax.

In truth, plenty was smoked before the Adams slaying and afterwards in an astonishing crime binge. For six hours before Baninzi's arrest, the gang broke into three houses and hijacked three cars. In between, they stopped at their Nyanga hideout to stash stolen TVs, laptops, cellphones, ATM cards and clothing, and to refuel on booze and Mandrax.

Back to the office where Jonathan is listening to Baninzi's confession. With it in the bag, Jonathan hit the pause button. He made some phone calls. Deliberately sitting at the table across from Baninzi because he wanted to see the boy's reactions.

Delft SAPS confirmed the Adams family murder. A serious crimes colleague, Detective Inspector Andre Erasmus, was already on the scene and grateful for the quick breakthrough. Yes, they had found 9mm doppies lying between Felicity, husband Marius, 10-year-old Shaune and Alex, 16. Yes, the guns could well be those stolen from Timothy Ndabeni and Sydney Molefe.

While looking Baninzi dead in the eyes, Jonathan instructed Erasmus to charge Baninzi, Nontshongwana and Malusi with all four slayings. The youngster sat up in his chair as he realised what he had done. He had sent himself to jail. But the detective could also see the boy didn't fully comprehend just how seriously he had implicated himself. So he decided to allow Baninzi to believe his own bullshit that Shadrack was the shooter, even though he had been fleeing with both handguns. If he thought snitching would get him a lighter sentence he was in for a surprise.

The last thing the detective was going to explain was that placing himself on the scene while guns blazed was tantamount to him admitting that he was the triggerman. Best leave it to his lawyer to explain the doctrine of common purpose.

Ultimately Baninzi would bury himself with his own delusion. But first, lunch.

Chauke had just arrived with fish and chips for three. They ate without talking. For Jonathan it was kind of weird lunching with a serial killer who, it turned out, was South Africa's youngest. But the detective was on a roll. By taking a break and continuing the next day, the boy would have plenty of opportunity to reflect and change versions.

Once Baninzi had downed the last swig of Coke, the Confessor Cop did an unusual thing.

'Come sit here, my boy. Here. Next to me.'

Jonathan didn't want Baninzi slouching on the other side of the table, away from his crimes. 'I wanted him over those dockets, right up close. I wanted the full horror of his actions in his face. I wanted him to see what I was seeing.'

At the same time, Jonathan admits, he was manipulating Baninzi. 'I also wanted to lull him into a false sense of security.' So he said, 'Kom, Asanda, come sit,' tapping the chair next to him. 'I did it in a way that said, "Come and sit next to Pa. Now see what you've done, my boy? But don't be scared because Pa is sitting with you."'

Talking to Baninzi in this way wasn't all manipulation. 'As I opened the dockets one by one, lingering on each crime scene, I saw the tears welling in Asanda's eyes. And I felt sorry for him. Yes, he was the cold-blooded killer who had haunted my dreams for months. But he was also just a boy.' A lost boy. 'In that moment I saw myself in him. I remembered my childhood pain. How I needed consoling. And I recognised that Asanda, too, needed consoling.'

The Confessor Cop watched and waited after closing his last docket. He had anticipated the next moment in his interview preparation after he left Baninzi to sober up the day before. Nevertheless, hearing the boy utter it was shocking.

'Tell me the colour and make of the cars, Mr Morris. Then I can tell you what happened there.'

Of course, the boy didn't require guidance, he needed to make sense of the sea of dead faces Jonathan had shown him. Some way of separating one nameless dead face from another. A reference point on which to hang the bodies that haunted his sleep.

Jonathan let the boy's question hang uncomfortably in the air. He needed a minute to deal with the strong impulse to place his pistol against the kid's temple and pull the trigger. He knew he had the capacity to do it. Fortunately, his pistol was locked away in his office down the passage for precisely this reason.

This isn't a movie, he quickly reminded himself, pushing his rage aside. He had to be Pa. The boy needed context. It was to be expected, he told himself. That's why the boy and Wox shot 14 people face down in the dirt in the dead of night. They did not want to remember their faces.

The cars, on the other hand, were fresh in his memory because they'd used them to move between crime scenes and had spent time stripping them for parts to sell. 'So as much as it sickened me, I jogged his fucking memory about who he killed. Or should I say who Wox killed.'

Because as the boy recalled each crime scene, always with the broadest of brushstrokes, he implicated Wox with the same ease he had Shadrack. Even though he always had a Walter 7.65mm in his hand. After each hijacking, robbery and rape, it was Wox who pulled the killer trigger.

'Yes, I'm sure, Sir, it was Wox,' he would say, slouching a little further down into his chair.

'I had hinted to Baninzi that Wox was a bad influence. But I didn't expect him to take me so literally.'

The repeated gang rapes of the women were also Wox's idea, according to Baninzi. Again, Jonathan suppressed his urge to challenge the boy's nonsense. His job now was to keep him ticking the boxes to implicate himself.

While Jonathan wrote up the confession, certain details triggered him. Such as Baninzi confirming that Siseko and Faltein, the dead men found on his birthday, had begged for their lives when told to kneel. Or when the boy described how he and Wox had hijacked taxi driver Richard Dantjies the next day and locked him in his car's boot so they could rape his passenger, Faith Qwelane, on the back seat. Afterwards Qwelane, the Sweats from Heaven cashier, who had missed church to work that Sunday, was driven to an abandoned shack. There she and Dantjies were shot in the backs of their heads. The detective remembers feeling their utter helplessness in an old familiar knot in his stomach.

Listening to all this required every ounce of Jonathan's self-control. He could cheerfully have ripped off Baninzi's head. But he was Pa. So he stayed calm, pressed the pen hard into the paper as he wrote. Baninzi reminded him how stressed he was on day 21 of his investigation, August 10, when the body count was 10 and he still had no leads. This time they shot the boyfriend first. Then they drove Linda Mbambisa to an abandoned shack where they were joined by an occasional accomplice, Garrol Bosman. Here all three raped her. Then Wox turned her face down into the filthy mattress and shot her in the back of the head.

In the early hours of the following morning, Baninzi recounted how he and Wox masqueraded as cops to gain entry to a drug dealer's house. She convinced them there was no Mandrax to steal, so they simply executed Nomvuyo Mtiki while her baby sat next to her on her bed.

But Jonathan did not allow these distressing details to derail the momentum of Baninzi's confession. All that mattered was that the boy place himself on the scene, even if it was as a passive participant.

After four draining hours, the detective was at the end of his patience. Now for the last docket. The boy described how easily they had duped Sergeant Timothy Ndabeni and Sydney Molefe for their guns. No, the boy didn't know Ndabeni was a cop. His body language showed he didn't care either.

Again, Jonathan suppressed the urge to kill the boy. But he kept himself in check. By the time he left the room half an hour later, he had the foundation of the plea statement that would later jail Baninzi for a long time.

He recalls driving home feeling hopeless. It wasn't just the pointless carnage. It was the motive that was beyond comprehension. The boy confessed that their hijackings and robberies were like piecework so that they could buy food and drugs. Drugs that fuelled a vicious feedback loop. And that they executed their victims because they feared leaving behind witnesses.

And the rapes?

The boy had no answer. But it was obvious and deeply disturbing to the Confessor Cop. This kid was barely a man by age alone and already, fundamentally, he hated women.

Could drugs alone be responsible for that? Surely not? What about the bullying at school that Mrs Baninzi had spoken about?

Too exhausted to grapple with these uncomfortable thoughts, Jonathan found consolation in a mission accomplished. The confession now neatly filed in his locked office cabinet would put this manchild away before he could do any more damage to others and himself.

Taking Monday off for a job well done was out of the question. The priority now was to nail Wox, dead or alive. Before he could kill again.

Chauke was more easy-going about it. He was convinced Wox would complete the job himself. And if he didn't commit suicide, the community would eventually corner him and set him alight.

But Jonathan wasn't buying it. Wox became an obsession. That's what happened when a case dragged on too long. And it led to some crazy thinking.

Of course, Baninzi was no angel but Wox was a catalyst for his madness. Jonathan was convinced that in some distorted way the boy saw the older man as his role model and had killed to impress him. For that reason alone, Wox didn't deserve to live. So, if it came down to the wire, he would shoot him on sight.

'I told Chauke we were dealing with a monster who needed to be stopped even if it meant that I had to break the law and become judge, jury and executioner.'

But first Jonathan had to find Wox. True to form, however, the bastard melted into the shadows again. Was he biding his time, Jonathan wondered, or unable to operate without Baninzi? Or deliberately taunting the cops? Such were the questions that tormented Jonathan each night before he fell into a fitful sleep loaded with nightmares.

By the end of the week, Jonathan's rage was on red alert. He hadn't been able to take it out on the boy. But as sure as hell he was going to take it out on Wox. Had he consulted the research, the detective would have realised this was a pipe dream. Baninzi's arrest was pure luck. Because serial killers more often than not stay hidden forever.

Jonathan tried to blow off steam by kicking down Garrol Bosman's door. And then, when he eventually found him cowering under his mother's bed, he dragged him outside by his collar and threw him down in front of the backup cop team. It took self-restraint not to beat the man there and then.

Meanwhile he was also babysitting Baninzi through several brief court appearances, usually postponed for further investigation. But nothing helped. Wox remained front and centre 24/7.

Realising he was losing his grip, the detective took leave. The break was long overdue. His last weekend off had been before his birthday a month and a half previously. But spending time with family and friends in Gauteng didn't put Wox out of his mind.

Even though he knew he'd be told the moment there was information about Wox, this didn't stop Jonathan phoning Chauke at three in the morning, asking him if he had any new leads on Wox. No matter how hard he tried, he couldn't switch off. Not even in his sleep.

Jonathan recalls a scene soon after he returned to Cape Town. It's 3am in the parking lot outside Bellville Police Station. One of Chauke's informers has finally come good. Wox should show up soon to free Baninzi. They wait and wait. Then there is Wox leaving the station. Without Baninzi. Now Jonathan can end the nightmare once and for all.

He's out of the car, gun drawn, shouting at Wox to lie the fuck down. The fucker smiles back, almost as if he's been expecting Jonathan. Then he goes for his 7.65mm. Jonathan shoots. In an irrational fraction of a second, he narrows his focus to his barrel, then he hears the bullet slam squarely into Wox's chest, dropping him on the spot.

Enraged beyond words, Jonathan strides towards him, righteously, marvelling at how effortlessly he is finding closure. Standing over Wox, he aims between his eyes. Only cowards turn their victims face down.

Die, you pig. Vrek, jou vark, he hisses, pulling the trigger. Again. And again. And again. Until Chauke drags him away, wet through, back into wakefulness.

Jonathan's endless loop of daytime anxiety and these recurring nightmares continued for two weeks after Baninzi's confession. Then he got the call. A tip-off had led Gugulethu cops to a shack in the Barcelona section of the township. Wox was inside, refusing to come out.

By the time Jonathan and Chauke got there, the local community were already dancing around the demolished shack singing, the dog is dead.

'His suicide was a blessing in disguise,' the detective remembers. Wox wouldn't be able to lean on the boy to retract his confession.

Two days later, Jonathan heard two passenger planes had flown into New York's Twin Towers. 'The bastard's now hijacking aeroplanes,' he remarked to Chauke. Laughter made it easier to cope with the enormous trauma they'd both endured. But deep down the detective knew it would take more than gallows humour to make him whole again.

By the time Baninzi came to trial in May 2004, Jonathan had investigated one of South Africa's most horrific mass murders, a gruesome beheading, the murder of a toddler, and the Shallow Grave serial killer. The previous year, that first confession had put Baninzi and Shadrack away for four life sentences for the Adams family murders. And here he was in court once more listening to Baninzi's litany of horrors.

Most of what Baninzi's advocate read from his finalised plea statement sounded uncomfortably familiar. But new details highlighted how economical the teenager had been with the truth.

For instance, Baninzi's first version never revealed the degree of his misogyny. Now he was hearing that while Wox was driving around with their first hijack victims, the boy had raped the woman with the barrel of his gun in the back of her boyfriend's

Microbus while he was forced to lie on the floor. Then Wox stopped the vehicle so that they could rape the woman repeatedly. Afterwards they emptied their victims' accounts at an ATM, then drove to their hideout, where he and Wox again took turns raping the woman repeatedly, pausing now and again to strip the Microbus of its saleable parts.

Jonathan was dumbfounded all over again. What in God's name had turned Mrs Baninzi's soft-spoken boy into a monster who now sat in the dock showing no emotion while the victim's families in the gallery behind him wept?

The answers still evade him.

His only consolation now and then was the judge's gratitude for an investigation well done. The warm embraces post-sentencing on the court steps of thankful families, all dressed in black because, they said, today was the day they buried Baninzi.

This, Jonathan realises, will fade with time. But the image that will remain etched in his mind forever was Baninzi, now 21, standing in the dock for the highest sentence ever handed down in a Western Cape High Court. Still blank-faced. But as the judge delivered 18 life sentences for 14 murders and four rapes, Jonathan's lost boy wet his pants while the gallery behind rejoiced.

CHAPTER 11

MURDER MOST GRAVE

January 2002 – October 2003

Four months after Wox put a bullet in his own head, on 24 January 2002, Jonathan found himself standing over an open grave with a serial killer who was quite unlike any suspect he'd ever encountered. Because, from the beginning, Zola Mqomboyi expressed an urgent need to confess. Immediately, the skills Jonathan usually brought to the interviewing table were nullified.

Indeed at the crime scene, Jonathan had to admit, he was a bit afraid of Mqomboyi. It was supposed to be the other way around. Undoubtedly part of this feeling had something to with Mqomboyi's powerfully built two-metre frame and his cold, dark, brown eyes. He was an imposing man. The detective had felt it in Mqomboyi's unflinching eye contact and his vice-grip handshake when he had introduced himself as the new investigating officer. He sensed it again in the way the 39-year-old allowed himself to be handcuffed and shackled before leaving his cell to visit his killing fields. Such restraints were necessary procedure but seemed a bit irrelevant. It was as if they both knew the detective might as well have been restraining Goliath.

This man could hurt me, Jonathan warned himself again, listening to Mqomboyi recount why he had dug a grave for Gloria. Gloria was no longer in the ground. The forensic team had removed his lover before Christmas, soon after Mqomboyi's 17 December arrest. But if anything, her absence amplified the

93

imagined rage that had unfolded here. Here where things could go horribly wrong. Here in the bush, off the beaten track, in the wind and ancient beach sand where the swaying thickets of Port Jackson muffled any screams for help.

In September 2000, a month after Mqomboyi met his new 16-year-old girlfriend, Gloria, he discovered she had stolen his ID document from the remote shack they shared off Rotterdam Road, deep in the bush, away from any Mfuleni neighbours. Mqomboyi, who was then 38, also suspected that Gloria was having sex with the Nigerians who owned the taxi rank stall where she sold sweets and cigarettes. He simmered for a week before luring her into the bush about 600 metres from their shack for what he called skokbehandeling [shock treatment].

Gloria became so desperate during the confrontation that she stripped naked to demonstrate she had not been unfaithful, said Mqomboyi with a chilling composure that struck an old nerve. He responded by smashing her head with a brick. Blow followed blow until she was dead. Then he dug her grave, wrapped her bloodied body in a blanket and buried her where no one would ever find her.

The story told, Mqomboyi waited quietly for Jonathan's instruction. Then he turned back towards the ruins of his shack and, seemingly unburdened, led the detective directly to the second open grave about 300 metres away.

Despite the two-metre-high Port Jackson bushes whichever way you turned, Mqomboyi's route was unswerving. He knew exactly where his dead lovers lay. It was unnerving, remembers Jonathan, wondering if Mqomboyi had returned to them frequently. Did he reflect on his power? Or did he pay his respects?

In the short walk to the second grave, Jonathan remained on edge. Don't get too close. If he gets his shackles over my head he'll snap my neck like a toothpick. Then go for my gun and take out Chauke and group leader Captain Talmakkies.

This is Marie's grave, announced Mqomboyi, jerking the detective back to reality. It was the same depth as Gloria's. Mqomboyi dug all his graves until he was hip high in the hole, even though, he later admitted, they deserved to be the regulation six feet under. This led to him being dubbed the Shallow Grave Killer by a SAPS serial killer expert. Curiously, the press never picked up on this. In fact, they hardly reported on the case at all.

By Christmas 2000, three months after he'd killed Gloria, Marie had moved into Mqomboyi's shack. His relationship with her lasted much longer than with her predecessor. But 10 months into their relationship, in September 2001, it occurred to Mqomboyi that his lover's friend, a sex worker named Martha, who was now living with them, had enticed her into prostitution.

Under the pretence of collecting wood together, he lured Marie into the bush, where he confronted her about her betrayal. Her denials were met with multiple axe blows to her head until she was dead. Later he wrapped her body in a blanket and buried her.

At the third open grave less than 20 metres away, Mqomboyi told Jonathan that by the time he returned to his shack, where Martha lay sleeping, he had decided that she, too, had to die. Luring her into the bush past her friend's grave, he axed her to death. And repeated his burial ritual.

In stunned silence, Jonathan drove Mqomboyi down Rotterdam Road to its Hindle Road intersection. From there Mqomboyi walked the detective into the bush to grave number four. He buried his men well away from his women. And he didn't afford them a blanket.

This was the final resting place of a man nicknamed Mans, he told the detective. Mans had stolen a portable TV and tape recorder from his shack. Months later, on 14 December 2001, their paths crossed in Rotterdam Road. Mans fled. Mqomboyi caught up with him and dropped him to the ground with one hard blow. After kicking and stomping on him, he dragged Mans half-unconscious about 10 metres into the bush. There he found a lump of concrete almost half a metre in diameter. Zola only had to drop it once on Mans's head. Then he fetched a spade from his shack and buried him.

Jonathan was a little shaky as he drove Mqomboyi back to

Pollsmoor. The last few hours had been troubling enough in broad daylight. He couldn't imagine what it had been like for the cops assigned to guard the graves overnight when the forensic team ran out of daylight on 17 December before they could all be unearthed. Now he understood why some of the cops were so freaked out the next morning they had to take sick leave.

That night churning thoughts about Mqomboyi's 'tour' made sleep impossible. 'He was judge, jury, executioner and grave digger of his victims. I could hear them pleading for their lives where no one could hear them. I could hear their screams. I knew their help-lessness. But Mqomboyi never spoke about that. It's like he didn't want to go there. And that played havoc with my head.'

Instead Mqomboyi had spoken quietly to Jonathan at each graveside. With authority. Righteous with indication. Certainly not with the gangster swagger Jonathan was used to. Yes, in his telling, his victims got their dues for crossing him. But he was no longer angry with them. Just grateful that he had given them decent burials. And now he was ready to pay for his sins.

When Jonathan finally fell asleep, he slipped into a peaceful dream. Mqomboyi was still shackled but dressed as a pastor. He evoked Sunday school images of Moses. He even sounded like a priest reading the last rites of those who had sinned against him.

Jonathan woke the next morning grateful that his suspect was cooperating. It would free him up quickly to get back to the cases of Muggels and Baninzi.

It was convenient that Mqomboyi had also confessed to most of the murders during his 17 December arrest on a rape charge. All Jonathan had had to do was accompany him to the remaining graves and make sure there were no more bodies.

Apart from being wary of the big man, he was intrigued by Mqomboyi's Jekyll-and-Hyde personality.

On the surface, Mqomboyi seemed a gentleman. And an hon-est one at that. 'Driving back from the graves,' Jonathan recalls, 'I stopped at a café and asked Zola (Mqomboyi), if I send you to buy cold drinks would you come back? With a smile he said, "I wouldn't ask me to do that because I think I would disappoint you." I was joking but he wasn't.'

Jonathan was also puzzled why Mqomboyi hadn't pointed out all his graves to cops who had arrested him in December. After all, Gloria's grave was so close to the others. And the fifth grave he hinted at after his December arrest wasn't far off. Why wait until the new year to come clean? What was he up to? What game was he playing?

The detective didn't get an answer. But he did get one of the easiest confessions of his career. A confession that came even before they went out to inspect Mqomboyi's graves.

It began with Jonathan telling Mqomboyi he had been warned that he was a dangerous serial killer. Which was why he was now in charge, he added. 'Are you really that bad?'

Mqomboyi broke eye contact, his gaze momentarily shifting to the view from the window.

'I'm not a bad person,' he replied in fluent Afrikaans without blinking. 'Most times I mind my own business, but Gloria and the others provoked me.'

'I told him he did not look bad or dangerous. That if he walked past me in the street at night I wouldn't be afraid. He liked that. He smiled and then looked down at the floor like he was embarrassed by the compliment.' The timing was perfect. 'Are there any more graves, Zola?'

The Shallow Grave Killer made eye contact.

'I couldn't work out if he was confused or just hesitant. So I drove my point home in my best don't-mess-with-me tone.'

After a brief silence, Mqomboyi rewarded the detective's directness. 'There are two more in the bushes.'

This was alarming but Jonathan remained composed, applauding Mqomboyi for his honesty. He was now sure Mqomboyi was playing open cards. He also understood Mqomboyi's frustration at being held in Pollsmoor's awaiting-trial section. The man knew he was guilty and wanted to be done so he could go directly to jail.

But as much as Jonathan wanted to close this case, he felt a little uneasy at being hurried. There was a lot he didn't understand about this killer's psychology. Maybe he still harboured secrets. It was time to call in an expert.

Just over two weeks later, on 12 February, Jonathan watched in silence as Captain Almarie Myburgh from Pretoria's Investigative Psychology Unit for Serious and Violent Crimes unpacked Mqomboyi's past. She was a burly woman who took no nonsense, so the detective didn't expect any resistance. But he noticed how Mqomboyi skirted his early Eastern Cape childhood, briefly mentioning that he'd dropped out of school after Standard 5. Instead Mqomboyi began his story when he was 18 years old and found work on a Welkom mine. There he supplemented his income by dealing dagga.

It was a matter of time before the law caught up with him. In the early 1980s, he served 18 months for dealing. Six months of his time was spent cleaning the Welkom mortuary. It was a traumatic experience, Mqomboyi told Myburgh. And I bet it wasn't the first trauma experience either, Jonathan thought as he listened intently.

In 1985, Mqomboyi moved to Cape Town, where he put up a shack near the airport and continued to deal. Two years later a client, Milton, tried to rape his girlfriend, Felicity, in Mqomboyi's shack while he was out. In the ensuing confrontation a few days later, he killed Milton with an iron bar and buried him 15 metres from his shack in a hip-high grave. The sixth grave Mqomboyi revealed in his confession to Jonathan was never found. Factories now covered that area.

Early in December the same year, two clients tried to rob Mqomboyi at his shack. He killed one attacker with an iron rod and dumped his body at a refuse site because he knew it would soon be covered by the next load. Grave seven was also covered by factories.

The smell of Milton's decomposing body eventually became so overwhelming that Mqomboyi and Felicity moved to stay with her family in Elsies River. Their relationship didn't end well. A year later, in 1988, Mqomboyi killed Felicity in a jealous rage with a kick to her chin. He handed himself over to the police and was later sentenced to four years jail but was inexplicably released after just five months.

By 1991, Mqomboyi was back in jail again on a hefty sentence for housebreaking and a separate assault conviction relating to a violent panga fight with his girlfriend's family. Come March 2000, Mqomboyi was on the streets again. The scene was set for his final act of unresolved rage when he met Gloria five months later.

At this point Myburgh called time-out for a break. But Mqomboyi was having none of it. He declared he did not want to waste time. So while everyone sipped their tea, Mqomboyi went on to repeat his graveside narratives. It was as if he was making a grocery list. No emotion, no remorse. Just the violent facts.

Mqomboyi told Myburgh about Gloria, Marie, Martha. Moving on, he then explained how on 14 December, before killing Mans, he killed a Rasta with an axe blow to the head because he had tried to rob him. The man who was never identified was buried in the fifth grave Mqomboyi had alluded to.

He also revealed that in May 2001, two schoolgirls stumbled across his shack while Marie was not at home. The 13-year-old Maruchelle asked for directions to the rubbish dump, where her boyfriend worked. Before showing them the way, they shared a joint at Gloria's grave. Mqomboyi said he became aroused and dragged Maruchelle deeper into the bush, where he raped her. When she resisted, he stabbed her in her arm and choked her until she lost consciousness. Her friend fled and called the police, who arrived in time to rescue the still unconscious teenager before Mqomboyi returned with his spade. Mqomboyi remained at large and abandoned his shack and built a new one deeper in the bush.

This time on the drive back to Pollsmoor, when Mqomboyi asked for his case to be fast-tracked with the prosecution, Jonathan agreed, convinced that the serial killer had made a full disclosure.

However, he remained curious about Mqomboyi's childhood. So he decided to tell him a little of his own upbringing. This brought forth more revelations.

From the age of six, Mqomboyi witnessed his father abuse his mother and have many affairs. One of the affairs ended in murder and a jail sentence that left Mqomboyi and his twin brother, a schizophrenic, alone with their mother, who turned to alcohol. Predictably he struggled at school, where he was teased and bullied, eventually dropping out to herd his family's cattle.

Jonathan was overcome by sadness and a familiar tightness in his stomach as Mqomboyi spoke. But he didn't linger there, fearing it would overwhelm him. Best put his head down and get on with nailing the bad guys.

His next interaction with Mqomboyi was almost a year-and-a-half later, in June 2003, when he drove him from Pollsmoor to Valkenberg Psychiatric Hospital in Observatory for his court-ordered assessments. During the drive back to Pollsmoor a month later, Mqomboyi told the detective that he had expected him to fetch him much earlier. Valkenberg was not a place for him. It was for mad people and he wasn't mad. Jonathan recalls feeling empathetic but later came to realise that this was misplaced.

Mqomboyi's examining psychologists found him fit to stand trial. But what they unearthed in the process was far more frightening than a mental illness. Jonathan only learnt of this during Mqomboyi's August 2003 trial and his October sentencing.

During proceedings the detective came to realise how economical with the truth Mqomboyi had been. In his haste to get to jail he was running from the horror of his Hyde personality. But under the steady gaze of weeks and weeks of psychological assessment, his shadow side was exhumed.

Mqomboyi had lied to Myburgh. That lie concerned the rape charge that had brought him into Jonathan's orbit. His story was that he had caught his girlfriend Busisiwe Nkqayi prostituting herself and felt she needed to be taught a lesson. Her screams had caused the neighbours to call the cops.

But the truth was that 16-year-old Busisiwe had been abducted by Mqomboyi on 13 December 2001. He had raped her and when she tried to escape he had throttled her until she passed out. She had woken bound hand and foot in his shack. Over the next three days she was repeatedly raped. Then on 15 December, the day after Mqomboyi executed Mans and the Rasta in an escalating spiral of violence, Busisiwe was freed by good Samaritans. On 17 December he was actually seeking her out to kill her.

'It shocked me to read about Busi again,' says Jonathan two decades later, unable to recall why her charges never made it to trial. But what really disturbed him was a portion of Judge Wilfred Thring's sentencing that he had blanked from his memory after the trial. Indeed, when researching this chapter, Jonathan would only believe it when he read the judge's October 2003 sentence for himself.

'The crimes which you have committed are chilling in their severity and in the manner in which you committed them. I refer in this regard especially to the five murders. As I have already said, in all of them, except one, the crimes appear to have been committed, to a large extent, in cold blood and with a measure of premeditation. They were brutal murders committed in many cases with an axe. They were committed over a substantial period of time of more than a year. In two cases, where the deceased was a woman known as Gloria, and in the death of the Rastafarian, it would appear that you mutilated the bodies. This is an additional chilling factor in these crimes.'

'It was shocking to read about the mutilations,' recalled Jonathan. 'I had no idea and get goosebumps every time I read this again. No wonder I compartmentalised it in 2003 after the trial. If I hadn't, I think it would have overwhelmed me.' Because, at the time, Jonathan was already battling his Sizzlers and Baninzi traumas. The last thing he needed was for Mqomboyi to add to them.

Unlike with most of his other trials, the detective also cannot remember the Shallow Grave Killer's reaction in the dock when the judge concurred with the psychiatric panel's assessment that Mqomboyi was a disorganised serial killer. That he would remain one for life because the likelihood of his being rehabilitated was non-existent.

Quoting the head of the psychiatric panel, Dr Sean Kaliski, who was also Valkenberg Hospital Medical Superintendent, Justice Thring found Mqomboyi would be unable to control his impulses to kill again. He was thus a significant danger to the physical or mental well-being of others. Especially those close to him. More especially women.

'Mqomboyi was consistently able to provide a matter-of-fact account of his actions and did not ever express remorse,' noted Thring. 'This and the apparent premeditated and remorseless manner in which he murdered his victims were ominous. It indicated he was a psychopath. The accused is declared to be a dangerous criminal and is sentenced to undergo imprisonment for an indefinite period. I direct he be brought before this court again after a period of 20 years for the reconsideration of his sentence.'

Thank God, the detective remembers thinking as the judge nailed Mqomboyi's coffin shut.

It's finally over!

But it never really is.

CHAPTER 12

I WANT MY MOMMY

July 2003

He was sure he would be able to bury her and never think about this again. Nosey neighbours had made trouble by telling the police they'd last seen her entering his mother's house. But the Grassy Park cops who came knocking were poor quality. When they asked him to unlock the spare room, they seemed perfectly happy to accept that he didn't have a key. Then the wife got difficult and told him he couldn't borrow her Opel Corsa. And this had consequences. It also meant that later he had to lift her small frame out of the boot when the neighbours weren't watching and transfer her to the boot of his mother's Nissan Sentra. One stop along the way and soon he would be at that open field near Pelican Heights where he knew the sand was soft.

Life was just returning to normal when the cops came back. They were a different lot, who were not interested that he had put her in the hands of Allah. Now they were trying to pin him down. There were a lot of them. He could hear them muttering in the corridor outside the detective's office. And it was confusing him. He was also afraid because he sensed these cops would have kicked down the spare-room door. But they had the wrong man. Soon they would come to see that and let him go home. And then he would have words with those neighbours who couldn't mind their own business.

Detective Jonathan Morris took the stairs to his fourth-floor office. It kept him in shape and helped quieten his mind. Baninzi's High

Court trial for the Adams family slaying had adjourned half an hour earlier but it was still in session in his head. As he exited the stairwell, he welcomed the distraction of high-ranking officers in conversation down the corridor outside Detective Sergeant Anna Cilliers's office. Something big was going down.

Cilliers, his junior, was struggling. Her 25-year-old suspect, Mogamat Isaacs, wouldn't answer questions about eight-year-old Sasha-Leigh Crook, who had gone missing a week earlier on 6 July 2003.

Sasha-Leigh was staying with her Ottery grandparents for the July school holidays. Neighbours reported last seeing her walking into the Isaacs home to look for her friend. But a search of the house had turned up nothing.

The docket landed in Cilliers's lap a week later, on 13 July, when a security guard found Sasha-Leigh's tiny body in a shallow grave alongside a Pelican Heights soccer field near Strandfontein. Within days Cilliers had arrested Isaacs, who lived with his mother. She had also collected a number of exhibits that were being prepared for forensics.

'I could see Cilliers was going to get nowhere,' recalls Jonathan. 'There were too many people around the suspect. There was too much noise. It needed a calm head.'

After a quick flip through the docket, Jonathan went to inspect the exhibits. He returned within minutes with a photo on his Nokia of the green countertop police had removed from the Isaacs yard. And another of a green fragment found on Sasha-Leigh's clothing.

'I'm no forensic expert but it looked like a match to me. I said to Cilliers, lend him to me, and led Isaacs to my office down the corridor away from the noise.'

Isaacs was nervous in the blue office chair on the other side of Jonathan's desk. So the Confessor Cop put him at ease. Isaacs was here to tell his side of the story, he said, removing his desk phone from the cradle. It sent the message that Isaacs had his full attention. The detective then closed his office door on the outside noise as if to say, trust me, what you have to say is between you and me.

Isaacs visibly relaxed. More so when the detective inquired if he'd been assaulted during his arrest. Such concern had Isaacs talking about himself within minutes. He was adopted at a very young age. He recently got married but because he was currently unemployed they were living with his mother, who was his pillar of strength.

Mine is too, replied the detective, mirroring his suspect. It was getting cosy in the office. 'I'm married to an Isaacs from Athlone,' Jonathan shared, mentioning a family member by name. He resisted saying, barely married. Isaacs eyes lit up. They were also his relatives! The Confessor Cop was in.

'I think he thought it was his lucky day. That because we were family I was his getaway card. In his mind, closing my door now made absolute sense. I just smiled because without realising it he'd dropped his guard enough to give me a way in.'

'Did you kill Sasha-Leigh?'

The abrupt switch left Isaacs nonplussed.

'Were you at home the day Sasha-Leigh disappeared?'

'Did you speak to her?'

I wasn't home, stammered the suspect. 'I didn't see her at all.'

'Do you know what she looks like?'

The detective couldn't be certain but he detected a flash of shame in Isaacs' expression.

'Of course I do. She's my neighbour's grandchild and played with my niece.' After a pause, Isaacs added, in the road. 'They played in the road.'

He's trying to keep her out of the house, noted Jonathan.

'Did you ever speak to her?'

'Of course. I spoke to her and my niece before when they played in the road.'

'Was the deceased afraid of you? Would she come if you called her?'

'There is no reason for her to be afraid of me.'

The detective lifted his eyebrow ever so slightly, noting it induced a degree of anxiety.

Time to turn it up a notch. 'The green countertop chip put her in your yard. She followed you into your mom's house. A white bucket with blood stains was found in the garage.'

Isaacs couldn't look the detective in the eye. He fidgeted in his chair as if he needed the toilet.

'It doesn't look good, Mogamat.' The suspect looked as if he was about to cry.

It was the Confessor Cop's cue to get closer.

Moving around his desk he placed his hand on his suspect's shoulder so that he would look up.

'It's time to tell the truth, Mogamat. If you're honest, I'll look after you. There's no need to be afraid. We're family.'

The detective was expecting the tears he unleashed. His own caught him off-guard. Quickly he excused himself. His spontaneous tears confused him. But all he needed was a moment in the corridor.

When the detective returned, Isaacs was sobbing. Jonathan quickly regained his stride.

'I don't know what came over me,' confessed Isaacs. 'It was the drugs.'

'It's okay,' consoled the detective patting Isaacs' back. 'It's good to cry. It tells me you are sorry. We all make mistakes. But you can put it right by showing remorse.'

Isaacs' surrender was complete.

He described how he stabbed Sasha-Leigh in the neck and kept her body for four days before driving to mosque to pray about her body in his boot. How he felt bitterly sorry when he buried her without her mother present.

The detective had to think quickly. He was still a warrant officer. The quickest confession of his career was not binding in court unless witnessed by a commissioning officer or magistrate. The workaround came to him suddenly.

'You need to tell your mother before you confess to anyone else. Your mother is family. I know she would want that. I'd want that if you were my son.'

Isaacs fell apart. 'I want my mommy!'

The detective stayed present while colleagues raced to fetch Mrs Isaacs.

'I didn't want to leave the boy alone for a moment. Or take him back to Cilliers's office. My seniors would panic him with their questions. Then he might change his story. My job was to keep him vulnerable until his mother arrived. It was a no-brainer how she would react.'

'Tamaaf, Mommy! Tamaaf!' wailed Isaacs as the detective led him back into Cilliers's office. The Cape vernacular way of saying sorry was heart rending, Jonathan recalls.

Falling into his mother's arms, Isaacs confessed while senior officers in the room listened. Isaacs was still weeping when his mother signed a statement confirming her son's awful admission.

Jonathan's job was done but he couldn't celebrate. Not in front of a distraught mother who had lost her boy. As a father, Jonathan couldn't imagine anything worse.

At 10pm that night the detective was woken by his ringtone, 'The Ketchup Song'. His annoyance faded immediately when he heard the Parow charge office sergeant put Isaacs on the line. He had vital information.

Could it wait until the morning, asked the exhausted detective.

It might be too late, replied Isaacs, hinting at suicide.

Jonathan raced to the station.

He calmed Isaacs, who then revealed where he had hidden the murder weapon. And then cried again with remorse. Jonathan had had enough. But he wanted this to go to court for Mrs Crook's sake. So he placed Isaacs on suicide watch and left to lose himself in sleep.

From that night on, the detective had nothing more to do with the case other than the occasional snippet from an ever-grateful Cilliers.

During Isaacs' August 2005 trial, he heard via the grapevine that the accused had done a flip-flop, claiming he had been framed, even though shocking post-mortem evidence showed he kept

Sasha-Leigh captive before killing her. His mother also lied to the court, claiming the confession had never taken place. But Jonathan didn't give it a second thought. He had seen his fair share of flip-flops come trial time.

Unbeknown to him, Isaacs was sentenced to life on the same day Jonathan was attending another High Court matter. At the tea break, the detective walked out of court into a bustling corridor. Suddenly a woman stepped from the crowd and slapped him sharply on the chest. Thank you, Mr Morris! she declared sarcastically.

For a moment, the detective was annoyed at the arrogance in her voice and the assault. As he was about to reprimand the woman, he recognised her as Mrs Isaacs.

'It was a shock, but I brushed it off without responding. It told me something about the home Mogamat grew up in. And I understood it was her messed-up way of grieving the loss of her boy.

But her behaviour hurt me. Finding justice for Sasha-Leigh was one of my proudest moments as a police officer. When the truth comes like that, it touches my heart. It's holy. I'm not outspoken about my faith. But I will tell you this. If ever God was working through me, it was the day Mogamat confessed. And He doesn't make mistakes.'

CHAPTER 13

THE JESUS LETTERS

April 2005 – January 2006

Repair them. That's the first thing Captain Jonathan Morris did when Provincial Commissioner Mzwandile Petros's office dumped a pile of 17 dockets on his desk three weeks before Christmas 2005. A dozen of them for murders and rapes that a variety of Philippi detectives had been unable to solve.

They were in bad shape. Their covers were torn at the sides, the statements were dog-eared. So Jonathan gave them all new covers, each one duct-taped down the spine. He could never work with a dirty docket. Sending a dirty docket to court was disrespectful towards a prosecutor. And it said a lot about an investigator's character and capabilities. If ever there was living proof of that maxim it was the context of this sorry mess on his desk.

It took the detective about 30 minutes to get the bundle ship-shape. Only then was he ready to begin the bigger, onerous repair: solving the most bungled serial murder investigation ever to come his way.

From the first page of the first docket it was distressing reading.

The terror began in rural Philippi in April 2005 with the brutal rape of flower farm worker Bonnie Swartz, who was attacked one night during a walk to the shops. The attacker subdued her with a rock to her head. Then dragged her into the bush, stripped her naked, tied her to a tree and raped her four times. Bonnie thought she was dying where he left her. But she hung on for hours until she was rescued.

Some three weeks later, a man matching Bonnie's description of her rapist ambushed Nolusindiso Sono in Weltevreden Road, Philippi, in the early hours of the morning as she searched for her lost dog. He strangled her to death after raping her.

On the evening of 7 May, in the same road, he spotted a couple walking home. Mina Jarvis hung back a while after her boyfriend entered their home. The man pounced, dragging her back into the bush where he had been lying in wait. After raping her, he threw Mina in a nearby farm dam and patrolled the edge to stop her from paddling to the side. Mina bobbed to the surface, then disappeared. Then surfaced again. Then disappeared one last time.

The killer paused all the way into July. But if anything his absence amplified the collective anxiety of the community.

Then on Sunday, 24 July, he broke into the Puntweg house of Lekkerwater Farm workers Sarah Slamat and Richard Cornelius. He dispatched the latter with a pole to his head and raped Sarah, traumatising her for years to come.

Almost as if he were making up for his hiatus, he struck again on the Friday of July's last weekend, this time in the bush near Westgate Mall, Mitchells Plain, where he raped Nella Tersia Links twice. That same night he stalked a homeless couple in the hills above Westridge. After bludgeoning Hilton Alkonsteyn to death, he raped his partner twice. She never laid a charge, but her story spread terror and panic.

By now there wasn't a Philippi farmworker who was not look-ing over their shoulder in fear. Especially once night came. When pleas for police assistance were met with no response, they formed a neighbourhood watch that searched the night streets and bush paths in vain. The police could not see it, but the farmworkers were adamant there was a pattern. They were being stalked by a serial killer from within their midst. He was watching them from the surrounding dunes and bush to pick his moment to strike. And then dump the bodies in or near a farm irrigation dam.

July was also the month that he got a nickname: Jesus Killer.

It was first voiced in a tabloid reporting an eyewitness claiming she had heard the attacker scream: I'm Jesus and I'm coming to fetch you.

This was embellished with the rumour that the words Jesus Killer were tattooed on his forehead. Or maybe on his upper lip and his chest. The only explanation Jonathan could come up with for these fake reports was that a nameless, faceless serial killer was more terrifying than one with a name.

Even though the killer was surprised, eventually and apparently pleasantly, by the nickname, he had no tattoos. But the moniker stuck. And it was so catchy that no newspaper dared report it as community-inspired.

The Jesus Killer went quiet again in August but surfaced at the end of September. The body count now mounted alarmingly and the serial killer allegations made the national news. However, SAPS remained convinced they were looking for multiple suspects.

After kidnapping 18-year-old Irene Adams on 22 September, the Jesus Killer raped her daily for two days before releasing her. Consumed by jealousy, the following week when he saw her in the company of another man, the Jesus Killer splashed a message on a wall in broad orange brushstrokes: KARIEN NAAI MAAR LEKKER EK KOM VIR JOU [Keep screwing around Karien, I'm coming for you.] The name was an oddity that would only be clarified months later.

In early October, he returned to Puntweg and broke into a couple's home. After drinking two glasses of wine, he beat Petrus Marks to death with a pole and dumped his body in a dam.

That week he also broke into the house of Koekie de Vos and Frans Mouwers and attempted to murder them. They survived. He got away.

On a Friday a few weeks later, he returned to the Weltevreden Road area, where he encountered a drunk Griet Koela. He recognised her as having been in the shebeen where he had been drinking and smoking Mandrax. He raped her when she refused to have sex with him. Before strangling her to death, he promised to leave directions to her body with her friend Tokkie so that she could arrange a proper burial.

Then he followed Griet's directions to where her drunk partner and his friend were passed out in the bush. They had money. He beat Howard Stuurman and Brendon Korokee with a pole until they stopped breathing.

On the following Monday, he called Mitchells Plain Police Station twice to tip them off about Griet's body. But come Thursday, flies were still buzzing around her corpse. He did as he'd promised and dropped a note with directions through Tokkie's window.

On the last weekend of October, the Jesus Killer went hunting for more drunk victims on Cape Seedlings Farm, off Varkensvlei Road.

Lucas Manewel called for his neighbour when he spotted a suspicious stranger peering through his window. The Jesus Killer dispatched them both. Afterwards he entered Manewel's house to search for money. There he found Miena Manewel and raped her.

During the early hours of the first Friday in November, the Jesus Killer broke into Marie Roman and Johannes Willemse's home on Kleinsorgen Farm. After drinking their wine, he battered the sleeping Johannes with a pole, then dragged Marie outside and raped her.

Two weekends later, after drinking all afternoon, he stalked a drunk couple down Weltevreden Road to their house on Honeydew Farm. By then it was dark. Alerted by his barking dog, Martinus Baniswa challenged the killer in the shadows. But his knopkierie was no match for the man's trademark pole. He then went after the woman.

By then Sally van Niekerk had locked her burglar-barred house and her bedroom door. But the Jesus Killer broke through the roof, kicked down the door and raped her.

On that same November weekend, he struck again at Geduld Farm, where he strangled Jennifer Petersen after raping her. He dumped her body in a dam.

Eventually, a week later, SAPS reacted to escalating community and media pressure that gave the Independent Police Investigative Directorate no choice. Police were now hunting a serial killer, declared a SAPS spokesperson on national TV, with no blush or apology. And a hand-picked provincial task team would bring him to book.

They made an arrest within four days. But they got the wrong guy. That's when Petros fired them and called in Morris to sort out their bungling.

It took almost the whole day. But by the time the detective finished examining the 17 dockets, there was no doubt he had a serial killer on his hands. And it wasn't the task team's prime suspect, Stanley Martens.

Immediately Jonathan roped in serial killer expert Dr Gerard Labuschagne. Then he recruited two detectives from the task team who were familiar with all the cases, telling his foot soldiers there would be no time off or rest days until the killer was arrested.

Together they revisited each crime scene so that Labuschagne could gather enough detail to begin compiling a profile.

Next Jonathan turned his attention to Stanley Martens. He had appeared twice in court for Bonnie Swartz's rape. Yet the task team had not even checked if his DNA linked him to the charge, let alone all the other dockets on Jonathan's desk. In fact, during the Jesus Killer's eight-month reign of terror not one Philippi detective had checked if crime scene hair and semen samples supported their multiple suspect theory.

Following his hunch that the Jesus Killer was still at large, Jonathan interviewed Bonnie Swartz. She confirmed Martens was not her rapist! She had told the task force that Martens was too short and tiny. Her rapist was taller and well built. He had to be to overpower her.

After organising Martens' release from Pollsmoor, Jonathan set about interviewing surviving victims. It wasn't easy. Their trauma triggered ghosts of his Philippi past. And the pressure for a result from the top brass was unremitting.

Then Sally van Niekerk gave him the breakthrough he knew was inevitable. Again he was flabbergasted at the task team's sloppiness. She told him she'd given a cellphone, left behind by the rapist, to the Philippi detective investigating her attack. Yet it wasn't recorded in the docket. Why the hell not? Why was it lying in the evidence room at Philippi? Why had no one listened to Sally van Niekerk?

Eleven days before Christmas, on Day 9 of his investigation, Jonathan raced to Philippi Police Station and took possession of the phone. Back at his office the unit's cellphone analyst, Lieutenant Colonel Piet Viljoen, announced that the silver Nokia 6610 did not need a PIN, only a little charge. Scrolling through the call list, Jonathan noticed a frequently dialled number. This is it, said an inner voice that was seldom wrong.

He phoned the number.

Hello, Daddy, answered a teenage boy.

The detective held his breath, bringing his index finger to his lips for silence in the room. The next few seconds were surreal.

My lord, this Jesus Killer is a dad. He has a child. A family. He's just like you or me. He's working nine to five, killing on the weekends!

As that flashed through his mind, Jonathan thought, you've got him! Damn, you've got him! He felt it was like hearing the winning lottery numbers and realising you had them all.

Yet he stayed calm.

'It's not your daddy, my boy. It's Jonathan. I found your daddy's phone. What's his name and address so that I can return it?'

Within 30 minutes the detective was flooring his new BMW towards Grabouw, a village on the other side of the Hottentots-holland Mountains. Darryl didn't have an address for Daddy but he said his name was Jimmy Maketta. So Jonathan promptly offered to drop the phone in Grabouw, where Darryl lived with his mommy. Instinct told him not to chance interviewing her over the phone.

By late afternoon, Jonathan was speeding back to Mitchells Plain in a cacophony of sirens from a 10-car backup squad. What he'd heard from Mrs Maketta was a painfully familiar story.

Jimmy was an abusive husband. He had stabbed her a number of times until she laid charges that put him behind bars for several years. Now, out on parole, he was living with his sister in Rocklands, Mitchells Plain, bound by Mrs Maketta's restraining order.

If Maketta was the Jesus Killer, his lair was just two kilometres from Jonathan's mother's Portlands home, where he spent a lot of his time, and just 100 metres over the hills from his Westridge house.

It would have capped a perfect day had Jimmy been home. But his sister Annie, fed up with her brother's drinking and drugging, had told him to leave, three weeks back. At first she was indignant about 20 or more cops crawling all over her house. But once Jonathan had explained the situation, she was horrified and helpful.

While searching through the granny flat where Maketta had lived, he discovered a half-empty tin of orange paint. He knew it would match the threat painted on the Vibracrete wall.

By the next day, the detective had Maketta's rap sheet and his photograph. Strandfontein SAPS also confirmed he had jumped his parole. But Jonathan remained optimistic. Even when searches over the next few days of Philippi farms and at Mitchells Plain off-sales and drug dens came up empty, he sensed it was because Maketta was in typical serial killer pattern lying low. It was a matter of time before the Jesus Killer moved again. And when he did, he would nail him.

Five days before Christmas, on Day 15 of his investigation, Jonathan woke with an overpowering intuition that today was the day. Morning surveillance of drug dens, liquor stores and old crime scenes ended up in Dagbreek Avenue on a Westridge hill where Jonathan and his old colleague Detective Captain Ivan van den Heever had a bird's eye view of Annie's Pappagaai Road home.

As the hours ticked by, they cracked jokes and talked about what they'd do if Jimmy Maketta suddenly appeared in their binoculars. Should they take him out if he made a run for it? Interrogate him in the bush where no one could see? Throw him in a dam and keep him there until he was too exhausted to tread water any more? Hand him over to the farmworkers' neighbourhood watch?

Jonathan's phone stopped the banter. He let it ring a bit to savour the moment.

'Dag, Annie, hallo.'

'Morning, Meneer. Ek weet waar Jimmy is.' I know where he is.

Running from their perch on the dune back to the car, Jonathan was laughing hard with Ivan behind him shouting, 'wait for me!' Jonathan felt like a kid again back on the Philippi farm.

Soon Annie was in his BMW, directing him above the din of the 10 sirens to a Constantia address where Jimmy was painting a house with her painter husband. The owners have no fucking idea, thought the detective as they raced along the M3, before cutting their sirens a kilometre from their destination.

Next thing Jonathan was reading the Jesus Killer his rights in an upmarket home. For a moment he bizarrely wondered if he had the right guy, even though a puzzled Jimmy Maketta had confirmed his identity. He looked so normal. Like he couldn't hurt a fly.

Then the detective remembered the crime scene photos and squeezed Maketta's cuffs two notches tighter.

Before heading back to the unit's office, the Jesus Killer led his captor, and a now silent cortege of cops, to where he was sleeping rough at Steurhof railway station. Curiosity nagged at Jonathan during the drive back to Bellville South, so much so that he wanted to pull over and empty Maketta's backpack right there and then. But protocols were there for a reason.

It was 7pm by the time Jonathan had the Jesus Killer at his desk, sitting across from him, eating dinner. Now he could finally search his suspect's backpack, where he found photos of the man's many children. Typical of any devoted dad, né? Until he flipped them over. The handwriting was all he needed. It matched the note that had led police to Griet Koela's body.

Despite the evidence, Maketta was calm, denying one charge after another. In fact, the guy seemed to think he had the upper hand. He seemed to think he was making the cop work hard. Actually, the cop was biding his time until the denials dried up.

Jonathan loved this part. The drawn-out silence before he revealed his first bit of evidence.

'You left your phone behind after raping Sally van Niekerk.'

Maketta stared down at the floor. He hadn't seen this coming.

'That's how I tracked you down. Your wife told me everything about you.'

Jonathan let the silence drag on until the only way out was a confession to Sally's rape and Martinus's murder.

I can't tell you any more, Maketta protested.

The detective let it slide.

Now Maketta blamed his wife for his woes. When he punished her for cheating on him, she ruined his life with assault charges. Nevertheless he forgave her.

The Confessor Cop went off at a tangent and for a while the cop and the killer swopped stories about their squatter camp roots. Then the conversation turned to family, and the detective slipped in an innocuous suggestion: If you still love your wife, how about writing to her explaining everything?

Maketta agreed. The detective promised a personal hand delivery.

Forty minutes later the Jesus Killer handed him two pages. With a flourish, Jonathan pushed Griet Koela's docket to the middle of his desk and slowly, deliberately, opened it to reveal the note. He placed this beside Maketta's letter.

Jimmy Maketta looked away.

Silence.

Until Maketta could stand it no more.

Right on cue, Serious and Violent Crimes commander Colonel Stanley Sibidla accompanied by commissioners Mzwandile Petros and Anwa Dramat entered the detective's office just as Maketta confessed for the second time that day.

The interruption changed Maketta's mood. Angrily he refused to admit anything beyond Griet's rape and murder and the slaying of her husband and his friend. He was tired and wanted to get back to his cell.

The detective smiled.

He had plenty more questions. But tomorrow was another day. He had all the time in the world. And Jimmy Maketta was right where he wanted him.

Jonathan only got home well after midnight. He'd been on the go since 5am but sleep wouldn't come. So he read Maketta's letter.

Janetta Getruida Maketta.

Dear with regards to my health things are going very bad with me at the moment do you know what is happening what I want to tell you is that all the years that I grew up things got worse with me.

I met you and you lived with me and you gave me children but still things did not work out between the two of us.

Netta the time you left me and that time I went in and out of prison a sickness like a lion or tiger entered my body and from that time I hated women and men.

I couldn't come right with people and just wanted to be on my own. Netta I am sitting in a deep case but the detective handling the case told me to tell the truth and then he can help me with my problem.

And my detective went through all the years cases against me and saw a man like me he gonna help because he saw the problem before I could tell him.

I put all my trust in him and will tell him everything because I don't care what is going to happen to me in prison because I am already here, and I also want you to tell my children.

When I was there on Thursday, I just came to greet you and the children, my brothers, sister, father and in laws.

I also want to tell you that you and the children that maybe you will never see me again in this life.

I also want to tell you I have a sickness that will make me die in prison.

I can't tell you about the sickness but if it gets worse later I must tell you and the children. I also want to tell you not to keep the children away from me.

Netta I want to tell you there is a reason why I did these things.

Netta the time I went to live by Annie I thought I was going to have a better life and she was going to help me with my problem but things got worse and I became all confused. For five months I drank a lot and smoked drugs because at Annie's house they lived like cats and dogs with each other.

118

I chose to drink and to smoke drugs and then I would walk in a direction. And if someone appear before me then I would destroy them. The time I lived by Annie I just wanted to walk because their house problems ate me up inside.

I also want to tell you my heart is very sore because I must live with other people while I have a house and you live with another woman's man in my house. Netta I want to tell you today that I roamed around.

I want to tell you, you must remember. The children know everything because they are big and as I roam around today and live in the bush it will also happen to you one day.

So go tell my children that I say I'm not dead, I live and one day they will see me again. I am going to rest a bit and when everything is over I will be reunited with them.

At the moment my body and soul need rest and it is now the time to give my soul a chance to rest because I'm like a wandering spirit that could not find any rest.

Netta I also want to tell you it was not my duty to say sorry. It was your duty to come to me and say sorry because all the things that happened are your fault because you never asked about my wellbeing or where I lived.

The reason why I am so confused is because you are living in my house with another woman's man and how must my children grow up. My children are wandering and you are drinking yourself drunk. I want you to find out which prison I am in so that you can bring them to visit me.

I am writing this letter so that you know what is going on in my life Netta. I will know where I am because in the last few days I have wandered a lot. I also want to tell you the day when I come out I want me and you to talk about the house and the children.

See you soon

From Jimmy Maketta

Jimmy's spidery handwriting was a challenge to read. Long sentences without punctuation and a crazy paragraphing style required repeated reading before the detective could make sense of the words. But that was part of this gift. By the time Jonathan put the letter back in his briefcase, he had the insights he needed for his next round of questions.

As he lay awake in the dark, there was little doubt that Maketta would remain onside. The detective's only misgiving was Maketta's reaction to his handwriting ambush. Would he be resentful? Or, like a child, would he continue to trust his detective?

Sleep only arrived after 2am and it was fitful. Yet when dawn came, the detective began his day fully energised. He felt Maketta would reveal more and he was grateful that his promotion to captain meant he no longer had to track down a magistrate to hear the man's confession.

It felt good that for the first time in his career, a confession he had carefully orchestrated was already in the bag. And that he would be able to testify to it in court. Now he could focus on a heart-to-heart with Jimmy Maketta, a chat that would demonstrate that resistance to further confessions was futile.

Over coffee and his homemade cheese-and-tomato sandwiches, the detective explained to Maketta that he would be examined by the district surgeon. One reason was to establish that his confessions hadn't been beaten out of him. He smiled as he explained this to Maketta because he knew that if he hit Maketta, the man would be visiting the mortuary, not a district surgeon.

During questioning, there had been many times when he could have calmly throttled Maketta. Calmly watched life ebbing from the killer's shocked eyes.

The main reason for the district surgeon's examination was so that hair and blood samples could be taken for DNA analysis.

'Jimmy, did you wear a condom when you raped those women you deny raping?'

Maketta said nothing but the detective could see he was beginning to understand his position.

Jimmy, did you know that we have semen samples from all the women you raped, even the dead ones?

No response.

But Jonathan could tell from the man's eyes that he knew he was trapped. It was always the eyes that gave the game away. Long ago Jonathan had discovered he could read a suspect's eyes. They never lied.

In the days leading up to Christmas, Jimmy Maketta continued to deny the other murder and rape charges. Even though, bizarrely, after an identity parade he complained that one woman had the audacity not to recognise him! How was that possible, he asked the cop. He had raped her in broad daylight!

Until then Jonathan thought he'd seen and heard it all. Surely sooner or later this fool would realise that his arrogance was an admission of guilt!

Instead of pursuing that point, Jonathan again changed tack.

Jimmy, you're a dad, né? You're a husband. Imagine if someone had raped your wife. Your daughters. Terrorised your children. Your neighbours. Your co-workers. Imagine they lived in fear every day. Never went anywhere without looking over their shoulders. That they got so scared they fled their home to live in the bush or a squatter camp away from the killer.

Maketta nodded that he understood.

'That's how the Philippi farmworkers have been living for most of this year. You know why the murders have stopped since I arrested you?'

Maketta kept still but his eyes said yes.

'We both know why, Jimmy. The problem is the farmworkers don't know what we know. It's Christmas Eve and they are looking over their shoulders wondering when you will strike next.'

Silence.

'You owe it to them, Brother. Be brave. I know you have some good in you. Show it. Give your victims peace and harmony this Christmas.'

Maketta looked away for a long time. Then turned and looked Jonathan dead in the eye.

'It would be easier for me to explain what happened, Meneer, if you give me pen and paper.'

The detective reached for a sheaf and a clutch of ballpoints he had prepared for this moment.

'Well done, Jimmy. The truth will set you free, Brother.'

Leading him downstairs back to his cell, Jonathan spoke about Jimmy's children and how proud they would be that their dad had done the right thing. That maybe his truth would help them forgive him.

Handing him over to the charge office commander, he wished Jimmy Maketta a merry Christmas and then drove home to sleep.

He returned to the cells on Boxing Day with Christmas leftover roast chicken and potatoes that his mother cooked better than anyone else. And back copies of the tabloids, *Son* and *The Voice,* which were still headlining with Jesus Killer half-truths.

Jimmy was grateful and seemingly at peace. A priest had visited the cells on Christmas Day and he had given his heart to the Lord. Amen, Brother Jimmy, said Jonathan, with a gentle bow of his head.

Then Jimmy handed over a stack of letters detailing his sins.

What a blessed Christmas this was.

Back in his office, the first letter took Jonathan by surprise.

Dear Mr Morris

Mr I am sorry for wasting you and your colleagues time on Tuesday and Wednesday and as time went by. I feel much better and my human spirit is back and the animal spirit has left me.

I also want to tell you I am prepared to tell the truth never mind what is going to happen to me because I decided to play open cards with you because I can see you want to help me with my problem.

And as you have seen from my previous convictions you can see that I have a problem in life that has been bothering me for a long time. I am happy for the way you look after me and the manner you are handling my case.

This is why I decided to tell the truth. Mr I also want to tell you the majority of the Phillippi murders and rapes was done from my side and the reason why I say so is that I know all the crimes I have committed.

I now want the people to live in peace in their houses on the farms because you got me.

Jimmy Maketta's honesty and willingness to cooperate gave Jonathan goosebumps. It felt weird coming from a serial killer, but the validation felt good. He was proud that his respect for a suspect no matter what his crime had triumphed. It would bring closure to the victims' families.

There was also no escaping the job satisfaction. Turning one of South Africa's most notorious serial killers ranked as one of the detective's biggest career achievements. But now he had to focus on building a defence-proof case for court.

That started with reading the remaining letters where Maketta confessed to eight more murders and 16 rapes. One letter that triggered Jonathan more than any other contained the description of Mina Jarvis's drowning. Falling in love with Karien ran a close second. Maketta had misheard when he asked Irene Adams her name while raping her. This explained the graffiti he painted in orange rage, calling her Karien.

Later during questioning, Jonathan noted again Maketta's lack of remorse even when reflecting on Miena Manewel's suffering. His face was a dry, blank slate from one crime scene description to the next. Zero compassion. No comprehension of his cruelty and its consequences.

So it baffled Jonathan that he still felt sad for Jimmy. Yes, he was a monster. But underneath the rage he was a lost soul, a father who would have to live with the humiliation and shame of his depravity.

At his next court appearance two days before New Year's Eve, Maketta's legal aid lawyer tried to stem his correspondence. But the confessor and his cop were too tightly involved.

During the investigation, Jimmy Maketta laughed every time Jonathan told him, no more letters, okay? Your lawyer will blow a gasket if you write again. He'll come for me.

The teasing seemed to egg on the Jesus Killer. It puzzled Jonathan as he had never encountered epistolary bonding with a suspect before. Was Jimmy just toying with him? Playing some kind of sick game? For a long while, the detective could not put his finger on it.

What he did notice was that Jimmy was far more at ease confessing on paper than in conversation. Perhaps it was his unconscious way of coming to terms with his incomprehensible shadow. In the solitude of his cell Jimmy Maketta discovered by pure chance that putting pen to paper quelled his self-inflicted post-traumatic stress. Eventually this process humbled him enough to attempt an apology to his victims' families.

Whether he was playing with him or not, Jonathan was grateful for the letters. Not just for their content. But because they gave him breathing space to process the horror before his follow-up questioning. He needed that. Joke as they did at every handover of letters, those that followed were no laughing matter.

The Jesus Killer had a long line of victims that went back to a weekend in March 1996 on Grabouw's Brookfields Farm when he followed a drunk farm worker home. He pounced on the staggering Ida Kleinsmith, dragged her into the bush where he strangled her until she fainted. After raping her, he choked her to death.

In another letter, he revealed how, in July 1998, he struck another woman from behind. This woman, Samantha Lotz, was carrying a baby. He thrust the baby aside, hauled Samantha into the bush and raped her while the baby cried. Then he choked her to death. She was just 16. In the letter detailing this, Jimmy Maketta wrote that he was glad the baby was rescued alive.

In December 1999, Maketta got drunk with his neighbour's daughter at a Grabouw shebeen. Earlier he'd vowed to himself that he wasn't going to let Louisa Goliath slip through his fingers. He'd heard she was sleeping around, so surely she'd be game? But she refused to have sex with him so he raped her. When she threatened to report him, he choked her to death.

Later Jonathan collected the murder dockets from Grabouw Police Station and interviewed the victims' families. That's when he spotted that Maketta had been named as a suspect in Louisa's murder. But the detectives never got around to questioning him. Again, sloppy work.

Jonathan now had Jimmy Maketta for 15 murders and 19 rape charges.

And then Maketta dropped another bombshell letter.

During December he had extended his hunting ground beyond Philippi. One evening he attacked a sleeping homeless couple in Kenilworth and dropped a concrete slab on Michael Mandla's head. Then he raped the dead man's girlfriend, who was in a drunken coma. After a few beers, he returned to rape the woman again.

He reported his crimes to 10111 from a Rosmead Avenue phone box. Then hung up in fright when the responder warned him not to waste his time as the police knew exactly where he was phoning from.

Here was another instance of bad police work. It was compounded when the police arrested the raped woman because they were convinced she had murdered Mandla. She was in Pollsmoor awaiting trial when Jonathan arranged for her release.

More was to come when Jimmy Maketta confessed to raping more than 10 drunk and homeless women in the Wynberg and Claremont area. Police stations there could not corroborate his claims, but Jonathan knew that the homeless rarely reported a crime.

Once the letters stopped, Maketta's old habits returned. On New Year's Eve, with forensic investigators and photographers poised to be taken to new crime scenes in Philippi, he reneged on his earlier agreement to finally point out all his Philippi crime scenes. He was no longer in the mood.

Jonathan kept his temper and calmly returned Maketta to his cell, reminding him that he was only wasting his own time. By way of reply, Maketta asked for *The Voice*. Jonathan acquiesced. He had noticed that Maketta loved the attention, especially the newspaper billboards.

Jonathan's calm and kindness paid off early in the new year when Maketta sent word he was ready again. In a strange move, his defence lawyer sent an attractive colleague dressed as if for a wedding. She consulted with a shackled Maketta behind closed doors and then announced that he was no longer willing to point out the scenes. Jonathan could hear his colleagues cursing in the passage.

Jonathan asked the young lawyer if she had come to take instructions or give instructions.

Jimmy Maketta burst out laughing. Let's go, he said, to cheers in the corridor and an angry lawyer who stormed off without another word.

After an exhausting day of pointing out his crime scenes, Maketta called it quits much to every cop's relief. He had refused to point out his Grabouw and Claremont crime scenes. He was done with collaborating. He wanted to start his time.

Jonathan had also had enough. There was sufficient evidence to put away the Jesus Killer for the rest of his life. So be it. He now wanted a long break.

Jimmy Maketta was a distant memory by the time Jonathan set eyes on him again in May 2007 when he testified during his brief High Court trial. Maketta pleaded guilty to all charges.

The court heard from Valkenberg Hospital Medical Superintendent Dr Sean Kaliski that behind this soft-spoken pleasant-looking face, the accused was a typical psychopath with no capacity for remorse. Rehabilitation was out of the question. And he would kill again if ever granted parole.

For a long time, Jonathan cherished Judge Abe Motala's praise. 'The court and the community want to thank the investigating officer Detective Captain Jonathan Morris for his sterling investigation. It took Morris two weeks to arrest the accused after he took over the investigation. Morris won the trust of the accused who cooperated which led to many unsolved cases being solved.'

State prosecutor Susan Galloway, best known for her 2018 prosecution of family axe killer Henri van Breda, also commended one of her favourite detectives. 'I am of the view that Captain Morris's conduct was pivotal to the accused pleading guilty,' she wrote. 'Thus sparing the victims secondary victimisation of testifying in court.'

Without any hesitation, Motala found Maketta guilty on 16 counts of murder and 19 counts of rape. He ruled out any chance of parole by declaring him a dangerous criminal only eligible for court review in 25 years' time.

Denying the defence's request for Maketta to read one last letter, an apology to his victims' families, Motala adjourned. By the time the Jesus Killer turned to the gallery it was emptying fast. One anonymous voice summed up the collective mood: Fok jou, Jimmy. Ons stel nie belang in jou kakpraat nie. [Fuck you, Jimmy, we're not interested in your nonsense stories.]

Undeterred, with the air of a celebrity, he removed a neatly folded typewritten page from his top shirt pocket to reveal the small black Bible behind it. The media were all ears.

I write this letter with a lot of sadness and compassion in my heart.

To all my victims and their next of kin who now suffer for the deeds I committed.

This is the only way I can show repentance to them.

I realise they won't just forgive me because that is human.

But I take courage that as the years pass it will be possible.

I realise that I should not expect that but I trust that with the grace of Jesus Christ it will be possible.

I know I must pay for my deeds and I deserve it and expect nothing less but again I plead for forgiveness.

I'm ending with this verse out of John 8-11 how Jesus forgave the woman who committed adultery. I ask the public and family members of my victims to try and forgive me no matter how long it takes thank you.

From a person who has found God.

Perhaps angered by the families' lack of gratitude, Maketta rounded on his old confessor bro on the way down to the cells. These cases were only the tip of the iceberg, he bragged. The surprised detective's request for an interview was slapped down. It's in the hands of the Lord Jesus!

Indeed it is, Jimmy, thought Jonathan. Indeed it is.

Neither Maketta, the judge, the prison system nor the Confessor

Cop had the last word. Instead, on the wings of divine intervention, it was one of the Jesus Killer's victims. Maybe it was one of the many homeless women he bragged he raped in Claremont, but exactly who we will never know.

During the first year of his incarceration, Jimmy Maketta was diagnosed with full-blown AIDS. Is this what he hinted at in his letter to his wife? Jonathan doesn't know, because neither the district surgeon nor Valkenberg Hospital reported Maketta had HIV.

Whatever the truth, Jimmy Maketta's final reckoning was slow in coming. He had a long time to ponder his cruel legacy. Two more years dragged by before he died. Alone. In a prison hospital bed.

CHAPTER 14

MURDER MOST FOUL

December 2006

Hundreds of vehicles were already parked on the field opposite Taliep Petersen's double-storey Athlone mansion when Captain Jonathan Morris arrived at 7am, nine days before the Christmas of 2006. Wading through a sea of white kofias and kurtas with a heavy heart, up the long driveway past queueing mourners, he showed his badge at the front door.

The upstairs open-plan lounge was crowded with the bereaved, but the detective quickly picked out his shift commander Lieutenant Colonel Piet Viljoen. Quietly he brought Jonathan up to speed with the previous night's investigation. Then discreetly pointed out the pock mark where the bullet that had careered through Taliep's neck less than eight hours earlier had ricocheted off a floor tile.

Viljoen's briefing put Achmat Gamieldien and his wife and baby in one of the adjoining upstairs bedrooms when his 44-year-old mother, Najwa Petersen, woke them. She was accompanied by a gunman. Achmat became panic-stricken but his mother assured him that no harm would come to them if they cooperated.

Odd, thought the detective.

Taking their cellphones and camera, the gunman gently kissed the baby on its head and then left with Najwa, who locked the door behind him.

Even odder, thought the detective.

Throughout the interview with Gamieldien, the detective kept his eye on chain-smoking Najwa sitting opposite him. Oblivious of the small group of mourners trying to console her, all her nervous attention was fixed on fiddling with two cellphones. At some point she felt Jonathan's gaze. In the few seconds that their eyes met, the detective got that familiar knowing in his belly. There was something off about Najwa, who mere hours earlier had witnessed her famous musician husband being murdered in cold blood. Nervous, not grieving, she returned to her phones.

When he finished with Gamieldien, the captain eavesdropped on conversations as he moved around the crowded room. He overheard that Najwa's marriage was troubled. There was chatter that she had stabbed Taliep in the neck nine months ago. That he was on the verge of divorcing her. Viljoen had heard the same gossip and was moving in on Najwa. He did it discreetly but firmly: he wanted her phones.

She gave him one but held back the second. That was her business phone, the detective later heard. But Viljoen was known never to take nonsense. Quietly he demanded and seized the second phone.

By now Jonathan could no longer ignore his growing claustrophobia. It was like being back in the Sizzlers house, except this time there were way more live bodies around him.

He left the Petersen house quickly, knowing he could crack this high-profile case, which was clearly an inside job. He knew he could turn Najwa if he set his mind to it. But he also knew he should not be on this case. For the first time in his three-decade long career, he requested permission to stand down. He had to, because less than 24 hours earlier he'd buried his father.

Their relationship had been fraught.

Jonathan was seven when his father, Cyril, abandoned him and his family. 'From then on he was dead to me.' Until 12 years later, in July 1977, when he came face to face with his estranged parent at his eldest brother's wedding. Without forewarning, Nigel had begun reconciling with their dad.

What made the shock encounter even more distressing was that the father Jonathan never knew was his mirror image. Not only in looks but in their matching beige suits. It turned out they both shopped on account at Boulevardier in Claremont Main Road.

His father was pleased to hear he was a policeman. But Jonathan was not ready to reconcile. More so when his father added that many of his friends were still cops. Jonathan's sorrow ran too deep.

There was intermittent contact after the wedding. Once when Jonathan was assigned by chance to investigate a case of assault on his father by a machete-wielding man. Again during a family tragedy in December 1990 when his younger brother Russell drowned while rescuing two little girls from a rip current at Kogelbaai. For two weeks the Morris clan searched unsuccessfully for Russell's body. It was never recovered.

That was the saddest Christmas for Jonathan and his family. It was also the last time he swam in the sea. And from then on he tried to work most Decembers to still the fear that personal tragedy might strike again.

But even though Jonathan visited his father more frequently after Russell's drowning, the emotional distance remained. He forgave his dad but he couldn't forget. Then in 2000 his father was diagnosed with colon cancer. More frequent visits created a deeper understanding of his father's painful childhood. But it wasn't until late November 2006 that true reconciliation evolved during daily hospice visits. By the time Jonathan's father died on 10 December at the age of 75, the bruised 52-year-old policeman was able to begin forgetting. And overlook the fact that the man who had abandoned him and his family financially did not make amends in his will.

After burying his father at Plumstead Cemetery on 16 December, his superiors could see the detective was emotionally spent. The Taliep Petersen case was handed over to Captain Joash Dryden. But despite his mourning, Jonathan could not let go. Instead he assisted his old colleague and friend.

Analysis of Najwa Petersen's phones turned up the name Fahiem

Hendricks. She had called him 10 times on the day her husband was executed. Hendricks owed her money. They were lovers. They were negotiating a diamond deal. Dryden knew they were lying about these details but he didn't have enough to charge them.

Hendricks's phone analysis revealed another person of interest. Ex-con Raasiet Emjedi. The pair were in frequent contact leading up to the murder, which by now looked like a hit.

Emjedi works for me, explained Hendricks, who eventually stopped ducking and diving when he heard how Taliep had prayed before his execution. Allahu Akbar, he had uttered five times while being bound hand and foot in front of his wife, who looked on callously.

On 18 June 2007, Hendricks gave Dryden his big break by turning state witness. He confessed that Najwa had approached him in November 2006, asking for a hitman.

'Are you mad?' was his initial response.

But Najwa pestered him with an offer of R100,000 – R70,000 for him and R30,000 for the hitman. He buckled and approached his boarder, Emjedi, to source a hitman. Emjedi took his time. This frustrated Najwa, who pestered her lover continuously on 13 December. She wanted him to kill her husband during a staged hijacking. Taliep was flying back from London and she was due to fetch him from the airport. On their way home they could be hijacked. That didn't happen.

Two days later she pestered Hendricks again to execute Taliep on his way back from Wynberg's Luxurama theatre. But Emjedi only found a hitman – Waheed Hassan – on 16 December. The decision was taken to shoot Taliep in the house. Najwa's instructions regarding the hit were clear. No one else was to be hurt. The hi-tech security system including cameras would be off. And she would buzz the assassin in when he rang the doorbell.

Jonathan came back into play on 18 June 2007, when he arrested Emjedi while his colleagues arrested Najwa and Hassan.

Two days later he joined group leader Lieutenant Colonel Godfrey Wagter and Dryden at 8am for Hassan's questioning. The man quickly confessed to robbery. But he had refused to obey Najwa's order to execute her husband. Instead he had placed her hand inside a folded pillow and looked on as she pulled the trigger. Suspecting Hassan had not gone to the house alone, Jonathan asked him to describe his route to Taliep's house.

'Start again from the beginning, Hassan,' instructed the detective. Listening carefully this time, he heard Hassan say, we travelled...

'Who's we?'

Hassan remained silent, then looked down at the floor, head in his hands.

Dryden and Wagter stayed silent. They sensed the Confessor Cop was about to close the deal.

It took less than a minute. Then Hassan said, Jefferson Snyders.

Jonathan arrested Snyders and had him confessing all before midday. Snyders placed Hassan on the scene, gun in hand. He, Snyders, had forced Taliep to the ground, then kicked him in the face before binding his hands with cable ties and his feet with Najwa's scarf. He smacked Najwa but was restrained by Hassan who informed him she was the client. He watched Najwa plead with Hassan to shoot her husband. Then he felt so bad he left the house.

Damn, thought Jonathan.

He had more than enough. But no confirmation that Najwa was the shooter.

It's not your case, he reminded himself.

So Jonathan stepped back until the accused's bail hearing on 27 June 2007.

About an hour before the start of proceedings, Dryden called him from his car. 'Boeta Me, please come. I need to talk.'

Dryden wasn't coping with his messy divorce. In the parking lot a short walk from the Wynberg courts, he broke down. He didn't have the strength to go through with the bail hearing. Jonathan had never seen his buddy in such a state. It triggered painful memories of his second divorce during the Sizzlers investigation.

Choking back his own tears, he convinced Dryden that his pain would be harder to bear if court reporters got wind of his personal life. With patience and the loyalty that cop camaraderie fosters, he walked Dryden back, figuratively and literally, arm around his shoulders all the way into court. There the magistrate denied bail to all four co-conspirators.

Dankie, Boeta Me, Dryden said on the way back to their cars.

Jonathan smiled. There was more to this cop business than just being a detective. In that instant he recognised that the compassion he brought to the moment was the same, whether you were family, friend or criminal foe.

Jonathan kept in touch with the case from a distance until almost a year later, when Najwa Petersen and her co-accused appeared in the High Court. As expected it opened in March 2008 with allegations of police wrongdoing that were tested in a trial within a trial. Hassan claimed his confession was beaten out of him, while Snyders alleged that Jonathan had tricked him into admitting culpability.

It was a time-wasting strategy. Hassan had written his own four-page confession as if he was writing a book. And Snyders was careless in his lying.

Judge Siraj Desai ruled in the police's favour and, eventually, in February 2009, put Najwa away for 28 years as the mastermind of a premeditated act of 'sheer savagery'. Emjedi was jailed for 24 years, Hassan for 25 and Snyders for 10 for armed robbery, as he had played no role in the murder conspiracy.

To the man, Jonathan and his colleagues were star witnesses. And he left court with apologies from Hassan and Snyders, and his reputation enhanced. For the Confessor Cop the trial within a trial had been a ploy. Ever since his first major confession in the early 1990s, he had never raised his voice while interviewing a suspect, let alone his hand.

CHAPTER 15

BROTHERS IN ARMS

September – November 2007

As he did most weekday nights after 7pm, Lungisa Makhanya met his university student sister Nontobeko in Swartklip Road, where the taxi dropped her so that she wouldn't have to cross the dark field alone. It was only a 50-metre walk along the dirt path and then a few minutes under streetlights to their Mandalay home. But it felt safer together. Until the last Wednesday in September 2007, when two young thugs appeared out of the dark, demanding their phones and money.

Lungisa panicked and ran when, in the dim light, he realised one of the muggers had a gun. As he sprinted along the path towards the nearest house carrying his sister's book bag, he heard a shot. The thug caught up with him as he entered a driveway. He wanted Nontobeko's bag. As they engaged in a tug of war, the homeowner appeared. He was armed and shouted at the robber to stop. But instead guns blazed around a terrified Lungisa.

Moegamat Kasu was shovelling sand onto his bakkie when he heard a gunshot on the dark field behind him and a woman shouting for help. Then he noticed two men struggling over a bag in his neighbour's driveway. He shouted at the robber to stop. In the same moment, he saw his neighbour rushing around. He, too, was armed. Then came the loud crack of shots fired.

Carleigh Noemdo, chatting with his friend at the kitchen table, also heard a gunshot and a woman's screams. His friend grabbed his gun and Noemdo followed him outside. He watched his friend run to the two struggling men. In the dim orange streetlight, he saw the robber fire point-blank at his friend.

That night Jonathan was off duty watching a movie at his mother's Mitchells Plain house when the alert came through from radio control: Officer down!

Standard procedure was to drop everything and rush to the scene.

As he jumped stop signs and red robots, the siren hopefully ensuring safe passage, it occurred to Jonathan that although Tennyson Road sounded familiar and he was headed in its general direction, he didn't quite know its exact location.

Swannie's house was close by. He'd definitely know the address. And his friend and colleague, who now worked out of Lingelethu SAPS, would be happy to see him. As he turned into Swannie's road, it hit him. When they worked together at the gang unit in the 1990s, he'd picked him up here so often for work that he'd forgotten his address. Then he realised the officer-down call was to Tennyson Road. And there was Swannie's driveway lit up by flashing blue lights. That was Detective Inspector Phillip Swanepoel, 46, father of three, under the blanket in the road.

Jonathan was barely able to park. Rooted to his driver's seat, he watched old gang unit colleagues milling about, some of them crying openly. His happy-go-lucky friend was no more. Never again would he be first to start the braai fire, throw off his shirt and sing his favourite tune, Hot Chocolate's 'I Believe in Miracles'. Never again would Jonathan return home to find dear Swannie in deep conversation with his mother, who treated him as one of her own.

Without quite knowing how he got out of his BMW, the detective approached the crime scene amid commiserations from colleagues he hadn't seen for ages. Swannie had been hit in the chest twice and once in the stomach by a .357 magnum, they speculated. If the detective wasn't dead when he hit the ground, the end came very soon afterwards. Maybe he would have stood a chance had Detective Inspector Noemdo not left his service pistol at home.

The raw facts stunned Jonathan back into detective mode. Soon he had dried his tears and was interviewing Swannie's devastated neighbour. By now Kasu was in shock, struggling for the words the detective required. So Jonathan was relieved when the Serious Crime Unit commander Stanley Sibidla arrived with Provincial Commissioner Mzwandile Petros and Western Cape Minister of Community Safety and Security Leonard Ramatlakane. Without messing about, Petros made his order clear. 'This is your case, Captain. I want the killers behind bars asap!'

I'll do my best, promised the traumatised detective.

'Not your best, Captain. Catch them. Now and quickly.'

The pressure was on. Not just from the top brass and all Swannie's colleagues and old friends but from Swannie as well. His nickname for Jonathan had been Baasspeurder [boss detective]. As helpless as he felt, Jonathan had to get a grip. Living up to his friend's expectation was the most dignified way to pay his respects.

By the time the detective wrapped the scene after midnight, he had vague descriptions of the shooter and his two accomplices. One had robbed Nontobeko of her Nokia 6111 while the gunman chased her brother. Unbeknown to Lungisa, the shot he heard as he ran had struck him in the leg. Jonathan hoped doctors would find the embedded bullet. It would identify the murder weapon and possibly accelerate his manhunt.

Nontobeko also confirmed other eyewitness accounts that the shooter had run back past her on the path after his gunfight. Followed by her mugger. Both men had fled to an unidentified getaway car parked, hazards flashing, in Swartklip Road.

Jonathan also knew that Swannie's killer had stolen his Nokia 5500 and his 9mm Z88, minus a round. That cartridge lay next to his body. At least Swannie had fired a shot before being hit. Jonathan hoped it had found its mark because then the shooter would have to find medical treatment fast. It was a potential breakthrough lead. The killer's cap found next to Swannie's body might also yield a DNA clue.

Jonathan was exhausted when he eventually arrived home at

2am after chasing a false lead. But he couldn't sleep. Now living with his mother while he got over his second divorce, he was careful not to wake her. But she sensed him in the lounge writing up his docket's investigation diary.

She went silent for weeks after Jonathan broke the news. She was Swannie's second mother. The rest of the Morris family were staunch Bok rugby supporters. When the Springboks played the All Blacks, Ma Morris's only ally was Swannie. So of course they were tight. Of course they would gloat, about a bokkie on its back with its legs in the air. Gloat for the whole bloody week after the All Blacks won.

The following day, Jonathan could not bring himself to watch the Salt River Mortuary pathologist dissect his friend's body. He'd attended dozens of cop murder scenes in his career but just four months previously he'd been put in charge of his first police murder investigation. Even though he didn't know the fallen officers personally, it unsettled him.

What had happened was there had been a 10111 call to investigate a housebreaking in Crawford, and Warrant Officer Martin van der Heyde from Lansdowne Police Station responded. Unfortunately, he made the fatal error of entering the home alone. He thought he could take the 26-year-old suspect down but was overpowered and shot dead with his own weapon. On his way out of the house, the suspect stopped Student Constable Johnny Botha in his tracks with several shots to the chest from Van der Heyde's Z88 pistol.

Loping to the police van with both police pistols in hand in broad daylight, the Americans gangster, out on bail for motor vehicle theft, calmly slipped in behind the wheel of the SAPS van as if it were his own and casually drove away. All this watched by alarmed neighbours. It wasn't merely audacious, it was also an indictment of the times. Criminals no longer feared the police. There was little reverence for the uniform. Policemen were fair game. And that meant the police had to psyche themselves up. Convince themselves they were tough. Invincible. But when a cop went down, especially with his own gun, self-deception had no hiding place.

Each workday was a real and present danger. And that inescapable fact had far-reaching mental health implications.

These insights registered with Jonathan as he stood watching his comrades on the mortuary slabs while the pathologist assistants removed their blood-soaked, bullet-ridden uniforms and placed them in evidence bags. He had to swallow hard not to vomit.

That's why Swannie's autopsy was a no-go. His murder brought the helplessness and anger of that previous experience to the fore.

Swannie's first memorial a week later, organised by a long-time gang unit friend, began sombrely. But laughter soon mingled with tears as friends recalled his mischievous, good-humoured nature. How could you not laugh when the congregation was reminded that Swannie's other favourite braai tune was 'Die Maan Skyn So Helder Op My Poepol' by Lente-oes-orkes?

The second memorial service in Khayelitsha was also packed. This time with colleagues and friends from Lingelethu, Harare and Khayelitsha police stations. So, too, was his funeral in Beacon Valley, where he was again hailed as a hero, this time by Commissioner Petros, who promised Swannie's family, while glancing at Jonathan, that the killer would be found.

The shooter remained at large for nearly three weeks before Jonathan got his first breakthrough. It came via his old friend Chauke, now stationed at Lingelethu West detectives. During a random stop-and-search of a Toyota Venture in Lingelethu, police had arrested a woman after discovering a Z88 in her jacket pocket. Zukiswa Mangaxaba later told the detective that the pistol had been placed there earlier in the evening by her friend, Luyolo Yuyu. Further questioning revealed that the Venture driver was another friend, Lubabalo Hlengisa.

Both names resonated. They had been on every station's most-wanted list for over a week after an informer tipped off the captain that they were linked to Swannie's murder. Three hours later, ballistics confirmed he was on the right track. It was definitely Swannie's pistol.

The race to arrest Yuyu and Hlengisa hotted up. Only when

Chauke called Jonathan two days later did the detective realise that the left hand was definitely not talking to the right. Hlengisa had been arrested the same day he questioned Mangaxaba. And he was about to be released because the arresting detectives could not link him to Swannie's pistol.

'Where's he now?' asked the Confessor Cop.

'Sitting in front of me,' replied Chauke. 'But unless you have any bright suggestions, I've got to release him.'

Jonathan remembered the cellphone service provider had told him that Swannie's and Nontobeko's SIM cards were still active.

'Chauke, has he got a phone?'

'Yes. There's a Motorola on my desk in front of him.'

'Okay, dial Nontobeko's number.'

Chauke did so, using the office landline.

The Motorola rang.

'We got him, Boeta Me! We got him! Can you believe that. The fool was using her SIM.'

Then laughter. Deep healing laughter. And the image of Swannie laughing with them.

Twenty-one days after Swannie's death, Jonathan prepared for his first confession by visiting Mr Hlengisa senior. The man had already lost two sons to crime and had pinned his hopes on Lubabalo, a social-work student at the University of the Western Cape, where Nontobeko also studied.

Mr Hlengisa senior was bitterly disappointed in his son. And this was the information Jonathan conveyed to him. Adding, 'your father said you must tell the truth.'

Hlengisa crumbled. He admitted he was the getaway driver, Yuyu the gunman. His murder weapon was indeed a .357 revolver. Their friend Keketso Ponoane made up the trio.

In the days that followed, Ponoane handed himself over and immediately corroborated Hlengisa's version. Jonathan was also gratified to learn that Swannie's shot had hit home and Yuyu was nursing a chest wound. A few centimetres to the right and Yuyu would have died.

Both Hlengisa and Ponoane confirmed that their partner was in hiding, but they didn't know where.

There was a lone Crime Intelligence Unit officer processing applications for call data records – known as 205s – to cellphone providers. It was a laborious process. Something that should take less than 24 hours usually took weeks. The system was so broken that not even a police murder could fast-track the process. Although senior officers were aware of the problem, they seemed powerless to change it. Crime Intelligence were a law unto themselves. About two weeks after Jonathan filed his 205 to try pinpoint Yuyu's location, he still didn't have his call data.

At the morning parade and briefing, the commander turned on the tracing team.

'Where is Yuyu?'

'Still searching, Sir.'

'Get out! Get out!' he roared, chasing them from the room. 'And don't come back without Yuyu!'

If Jonathan had been investigating one or two cases, waiting for Yuyu's cellphone report would have driven him nuts. But he was always on the go, assisting the unit here, supporting colleagues there. Then back to investigating his own cases, preparing for court, appearing in court. A perpetual treadmill of busyness. Frequently he had to drop everything when emergency calls came in.

Such as the day a detective was shot dead outside Woodstock Police Station. A suspect was arrested. The cops had to be restrained from assaulting him.

'Give him to Morris!' bellowed the commander.

So Jonathan promised to protect the suspect if he gave up his accomplice in the shooting. Soon the whole unit was trailing Jonathan's BMW. But it turned out to be the wrong address.

'Okay,' Jonathan said to the suspect, 'one more chance or I let the pack in here.'

Twenty minutes later, 10 cars quietly locked down the suspect's unlikely hideout, a Philippi drug rehab centre. And here the man was arrested.

Job done. Until the next call.

More than a month later, Yuyu's cellphone report was still outstanding when an informer revealed that he was hiding in Ginsberg, his Eastern Cape home village. Within days he was arrested and by the evening of 19 November he was in Bellville South Police Station cells.

The following morning at 4am, Jonathan signed Yuyu out. He had imagined he was going to be confronted by a tough, swaggering young thug. Instead here was this skinny kid, petrified, out of his depth. Another lost boy.

As much as the Confessor Cop resisted it, Yuyu broke his heart. Although he was dealing with the killer of his friend, he felt more sadness than anger. He welcomed the short, silent walk across the courtyard to the Serious Crimes building and up the stairs to his second-floor office. It gave him time to compose himself and smell Yuyu's fear.

He used it. His tone was harsh, a little unkind. He meant business.

Yuyu nodded, cringed, as if expecting blows to follow.

'I've got no time for any nonsense!'

Then Jonathan laid out his case. It was ever thus. By the time you sat down in Jonathan's confessional there was no place to hide.

Truth be told, he had more than enough evidence already to put Yuyu away for a long time. But that wasn't good enough. He wanted the kid to confess. He wanted this for Swannie's sake, not just his own.

Yes, he felt sorry for Yuyu, a part-time bartender who had fathered a child too early in life. But he needed to be punished for his actions.

With little prompting, Yuyu confessed.

It took three years for the case to get to court. And along the way there were the usual legal shenanigans from the defence. The accused were not read their rights. They were denied their rights to lawyers. Confessions were beaten out of them. Confessions were scripted by the cops.

These were tactics Jonathan anticipated. Consequently he ensured that every confession was repeated to officers with no connection to him or the case. The same with the incriminating pointings-out. Consequently, the judge dismissed the accused's allegations, eventually finding them guilty of murder and robbery. But he showed mercy, deviating from the prescribed life sentence for the murder of a policeman because they were young first offenders with rehabilitation potential.

Swannie's wife, Ingrid, wanted harsher sentences and some colleagues also found the leniency difficult to swallow. But Jonathan was content that Hlengisa got 16 years, Ponoane 18, and Yuyu 24 years.

The case might have been closed to Swannie's liking. But what would have pleased him more was that he was not forgotten. To this day, war stories and jokes still abound.

One sums up his inimitable character better than any other. It speaks of loyalty and friendship forged in the crucible of trauma.

When Jonathan arrived at the gang unit's Bellville South offices in December 1994, he found it nestled in an animal farm under the blue gum trees. Scores of chickens, ducks, geese, rabbits and donkeys wandered around. There was even a fishpond and a vegetable garden. Jonathan had never seen anything like it since his Philippi childhood. He quickly discovered that feeding and caring for the animals was powerful therapy for the endless cycle of gang violence investigations. So, too, was the calming cluck-clucking and quack-quacking in the background.

The farm was particularly therapeutic over weekends when the detective was catching up with his admin. It had something to do with the familiar sound of colleagues' children running free among the animals and the smell and camaraderie of late-Sunday-afternoon braais.

The only disturbance to the peace was the farm's self-appointed bodyguard, the most senior goose with no name. He was tolerable while he was protecting the poultry. But he cooked his own goose when he began pecking everyone in range.

Swannie decided to make a meal of it. At first his trusted friends who fought hardened gangsters with him day in and day out found it hilarious. But Swakes, as he was also known, was dead serious.

Late one night he led an 'intervention unit' that kidnapped the gangster goose. Without further ado it landed up in Swannie's freezer.

To the mirth of the abductors, their unit commander launched a goose hunt the following morning. The insider joke that went to the grave with Swannie was that he and his gang were a key part of the day-long wild-goose chase. And it was Swakes who finally manged to convince his superiors that the neighbourhood dogs were the likely suspects.

Several days later, Swannie and his co-conspirators feasted amid much laughter on a delicious goose potjie at the Block House on Monwabisi Beach.

The goose wasn't the only animal that went missing. After a year at the unit, Jonathan decided he wanted his very own pet. He loved horses, so he bought a black-and-white pony and named it Brother.

The two quickly bonded. But Brother had a habit of wandering. People from the surrounding community would kindly return him to Jonathan. But Brother continued going on walkabouts. It seemed that he could not settle. As if he was a lost boy. Five months later Brother disappeared, never to return.

It saddened the Confessor Cop, who for some time remained on the lookout for Brother. Losing someone close was never easy. Especially if it felt like part of you.

PART 3

THE COP'S CONFESSION

CHAPTER 16

TWO PENS AND A BRAAI

It was inevitable. Eventually our WhatsApp interview sessions would reach that day in Jonathan's story when he buckled. When he could no longer handle the blood and gore. That day was Friday, 16 October 2015. When his workaholism stalled in a pool of blood. Literally.

A tip-off had come in that Giant Sweets in Epping were to be robbed. Jonathan and his team positioned themselves close by at a McDonald's near GrandWest. They would move to the factory as soon as the task force apprehended the suspects and secured the scene.

'Suddenly it was Guy Fawkes,' remembers Jonathan. 'There were dozens of shots. It was a helluva gunfight.'

Racing to the scene, he found one wounded suspect lying in a pool of blood and scattered cartridges next to a bullet-ridden white Mercedes getaway car with three bodies inside.

'The suspects made the fatal mistake of drawing their guns when ordered to surrender. There was no holding back by the task force. All the robbers were shot in the head multiple times with R5s. Blood and brains and bone fragments were splattered all over the cabin. It was not a nice sight. It was one of those really messy scenes.'

Jonathan processed the crime scene on autopilot as he had hundreds of times before. But that night he could not sleep.

'The dead bodies and wounds kept flashing through my mind. The next morning I said, ek kan nie meer nie, and quit.'

Office politics also added to Jonathan's disenchantment, his 'gat-volness'. During his drawn-out 11-month notice period, his close friend and colleague Lieutenant Colonel Godfrey Wagter tried to motivate him to hang in there until he turned 60.

'But I told him my passion was gone. It wasn't worth it any more. I had been working my arse off for too long, making myself sick, while colleagues who never went the extra mile like I did were getting promoted. I was die gewillige perd wat altyd geslaan is. [The willing horse that's always treated badly.] Fuck them. Fuck them all. It was time to quit. I was gatvol.'

Over the previous five years, Jonathan had become increasingly frustrated with the incompetency that unfolded when Serious and Violent Crimes had to integrate with the disbanded Scorpions. 'Some were sergeants and warrant officers when they joined the Scorpions with very little experience of serious violent crimes. But they came back to us as fucking colonels! They were the people who frustrated me the most. I will not be led by the blind. Not all of them, but I would say three-quarters of them were useless. They had no clue what was going on but they called themselves commanders. To be honest, it got so bad that when I travelled to work and saw the building I wanted to make a U-turn and go home. These guys had fokkol leadership skills and to make it worse used bullying tactics to compensate.

'Then there were sergeants who had only been with us for five years when they were promoted to captains. Some of them could not take a decent statement from a witness. They leapfrogged to captain and lacked the essential experience you only get from years of investigations. The traditional promotion route is from sergeant to warrant officer to lieutenant to captain. After decades as a junior detective, it took me 15 years to be promoted from sergeant to warrant officer to captain. You had to earn your stripes.

'But this bunch of palookas were earning big money for shoddy work. It was hard to stomach, especially when you had to fix their incompetence.'

For Jonathan this was no more tolerable than the racial

discrimination he had experienced throughout his career, especially as a rookie. 'I've always judged colleagues on merit, not the colour of their skin. That goes for everyone, suspects as well.'

Eleven months after the Giant Sweets bloodbath, on Friday, 30 September 2016, as a favour for a colleague, Jonathan questioned a suspect in the shooting of a Metro cop. It was a limp swan-song to a dramatic career. Seven months short of his 40th year in the service, at the age of 58, the Confessor Cop then packed up his personal belongings. Without saying a word to anyone, he climbed into Captain Viljoen Heunis's white bakkie for his last lift home with his Gordon's Bay colleague.

'Heunis was a real chatterbox and spoke nonstop. Me, I kept quiet. It was the saddest day of my life. I had no words. I kept thinking about tomorrow morning and not having to get up early for work. I knew I had made the right decision. But it messed with my head that four decades of my life were ending like any other day. And that the only person aware of it was me.'

Jonathan did not want to attend his own farewell party when he heard a few weeks later that his former unit commander Colonel Renier du Preez had arranged a farewell celebration for him and Wagter. But he changed his mind when he heard advocates Shareen Riley and John Ryneveldt would be there.

'Me and Wagter were tight with them. We became good friends after working on the Najwa Petersen case, and the respect and companionship grew from one investigation to the next. We often had lunch at Nandos together and I'm still in contact with them. They know they can always call on me for assistance. We know what makes each other tick and what we go through for justice.'

On the surface, Jonathan's farewell was pleasant. There was more than enough food. Colonel du Preez thanked him and Wagter for their service. And Jonathan paid tribute to fallen comrades during his speech, expressing gratitude that he was still around to enjoy his retirement.

Gifts followed the speeches. Flowers for Jonathan's wife, Leonore, and for him a pair of black Balmain pens engraved with his service dates and the words 'SVC SALUTE'.

They were beautiful gifts, he acknowledges, not wanting to appear ungrateful. But they held no meaning. 'I still feel the emptiness I felt then. On the surface I enjoyed the day and the company. But underneath it felt cold. I wanted my own farewell party, not a shared one. Don't get me wrong. I appreciated those who attended my farewell. But most of them didn't know me well. I missed the admin staff and colleagues who had been in the trenches with me for years, some of them decades. I did not want to leave in that fashion, but it is what it is. Water under the bridge. After the speeches I had one more beer and left. It was over.'

'What do you mean over?'

Exploring the wound is not easy for the hard-nosed detective whose pattern is to numb emotions and just get on with it. The hurt, which he interprets as self-pity, is not easily accessed. Ironically the Confessor Cop has to be invited to reflect. Actually, he has to be dragged there, soundlessly kicking and screaming.

'Two pens and a braai,' he says, biting back long-overdue tears.

The bittersweet irony is Jonathan treated his suspects with more respect and dignity than the police service treated him.

'It was unfair. I worked so long and hard. Two pens and a braai. That's not the way I saw 40 years of my life ending.'

CHAPTER 17

MEDALS

Despite all the interviews about his cases, I still wanted to know who was this guy, Captain Jonathan Morris? For one thing, why did he have no medals to show for his 10, 20, 30 years of service? He found out they had been issued but no one could tell him where they were.

Some three years before his retirement, while serving at the Hawks in Bellville, he decided to track down his medals. At the human resources department, he encountered a disinterested admin clerk who said she'd look into it. A few weeks later, when he hadn't heard from her, he went round to find out what was going on.

'It was embarrassing to experience that in front of 10 of her colleagues. There was no acknowledgment that this was important to me, no apology.'

Instead she wanted to know why he was concerned about the medals.

Because Jonathan didn't like confrontation, especially with a woman, he just walked away, seething. Behind him the clerk mumbled she would make more inquiries. But three weeks later he learnt that she'd quit.

It was soon apparent that he was not the only one she had treated with disdain. Her drawers contained medals for other members, but none of his.

'It's hard to swallow. Still, today. I loved my job. I don't believe I would have got as much job satisfaction in any other career. But it would have been a cherry on the top to get those medals and celebrate at the medal ceremonies with family and colleagues.'

At least medals would have been a tangible acknowledgement of Jonathan's loyalty and his sacrifices. 'They would have shown that I served my people with pride. They would have made my family proud. All they have now is my word that I was worthy.'

'You mean all you have is your stories with nothing on the wall to back them up? Nothing up there saying, you see guys, this is who I am?'

'Presies! Exactly.'

To this day, when he visits retired cop friends and sees their medals, he feels as if salt is being rubbed in his wounded self-worth. 'I suffered in silence. I just thought, where did I go wrong? There were cops who did not work nearly as hard as I did but they received medals. It really ended kak. There's a lot of anger and bitterness. I felt I was disrespected. My own people failed me. The stations where I worked should've informed me of the medals or sent them on to the units where I was working.'

Jonathan never complained to his commanding officers about his missing medals. Or about not receiving the R5,000 bonus Commissioner Mzwandile Petros recommended following his Sizzlers convictions. Or the commendation certificate that disgraced National Commissioner Jackie Selebi failed to sign off.

'I didn't have time for drama. I was too busy with investigations.'

This allowed the memories to linger with mixed emotions. 'I miss the colleagues who added value. The admin staff and officers who had my back. The men and women I trusted with my life.'

Most of all, though, Jonathan missed the thrill of the investigation.

'It was fun turning a dead case into a court case. Getting into the head of a criminal who thought he knew it all and then his giving me a confession. But what I lived for wasn't the commendations or the headlines but that feeling I got after a conviction. Money can't buy that. Every one of them will stay with me for the rest of my life. The closure I got for the families who were victims of crime is what kept my passion burning.'

Jonathan trails off wistfully. 'I also loved testifying in the High

Court. I got a lot of pleasure working with the National Prosecuting Authority. I believe I earned the respect of prosecutors and a lot of defence advocates as well.'

From his scrapbook in his kist at the bottom of his bed, Jonathan pulls a NPA commendation from Sizzlers prosecutor Anthony Stephen. Sent to Commissioner Petros, it carries the seal of Western Cape Director of Public Prosecutions, Rodney de Kock, who was the NPA's second in command until his death in December 2024.

'The investigating officer in this matter, Detective Inspector Jonathan Morris, is to be most highly commended for his investigation and assistance in this matter. This case was, without doubt, the worst case that I have prosecuted during my career. In order to appreciate fully the efforts of Detective Inspector Morris (and indeed his whole team) it is necessary to traverse some aspects of this matter.

'The massacre was reported internationally. The local media, unsurprisingly, sensationalised the matter which was immediately enveloped in wild rumour and speculation. The effect on the local gay community was traumatic and there was much speculation about whether it was a hate crime fuelled by homophobia.

'It was into this situation that Detective Inspector Morris stepped. It is to his credit that he investigated the matter as calmly as he did. Early on he realised that the solution to the case lay with the sole survivor and not with trying to chase after rumour and speculation.

'He gained the trust of Quinton Taylor and that of the gay community which in itself was remarkable, given the less than happy historical relationship that has existed between the community and the police.

'The result was that the case was solved in less than a month and the two accused arrested. Both accused made statements to magistrates confessing their involvement in the massacre and pointed out scenes to police officers.

'The docket that was given to me was a model of what a murder docket should be. The trial itself was set down for a month. Detective Inspector Morris arranged all the consultations tirelessly. He also made all the necessary arrangements with the Witness Protection Unit for Quinton Taylor to be brought through for consultation and also during the trial. It was thanks to his good organisation that the trial never had to be adjourned because a witness was unavailable.

'During the trial itself Detective Inspector Morris did all sorts of favours for me which helped enormously in reducing the stress of what was a very traumatic trial. One must also bear in mind that during the trial there were all manner of additional stress factors: the emotions of the families who were involved and enormous media coverage which was not always conducted sensitively or correctly. All these additional burdens were managed professionally. It was also remarkable that not a single witness was reluctant to testify despite the sometimes embarrassing nature of their evidence.

'The defence prevaricated about what they intended to do until five minutes before the trial was due to start. It was no doubt their realisation that Detective Inspector Morris had prepared an unanswerable case against them that ultimately led them to placing very little in dispute.

'It was clear Detective Inspector Morris had at all times treated the accused with respect and followed correct procedure. The statements that the two accused had made to magistrates as well as the pointing out what they had done with the police were unassailable.

'Detective Inspector Morris gave evidence in the closing stages of the trial and it was clear that the Judge was greatly impressed by the calm and measured way in which he testified.

'A record nine life sentences (in addition to various other terms of imprisonment) were imposed in respect of each accused.

'Although the credit for the success of this case must be shared by all the members of Detective Inspector Morris's team, I consider it fair to single out Inspector Jacobs from the Criminal Record Centre who was responsible for most of the photographs and video footage. This included the photographs taken during the nine post-mortem examinations that were conducted. It could not have been a pleasant task. All the necessary copies of the photographs and plans were prepared faultlessly. Inspector Jacobs also took the trouble to arrange for the plan of the scene to be projected onto a screen in court in order to facilitate the presentation of the evidence. The efficiency with which all the audio-visual evidence was arranged also contributed to the smooth conduct of the trial.

'Detective Inspector Morris and his team are to be congratulated on a remarkable achievement.'

Jonathan left an enduring mark on the NPA where several seasoned prosecutors still sing his praises.

'I still get phone calls from detectives when they hit a problem. I'm always happy to help with input and advice,' he told me.

It helped Lieutenant Colonel Stefanus Jooste while investigating the 2022 murder of Vredenburg Magistrate Romay van Rooyen in her Marina da Gama home.

'I'm still his senior,' jokes Jonathan about his last partner at Serious Crimes. 'I taught him. No, seriously, he hit a snag and we discussed his case like we used to. Together we dotted the i's and crossed the t's and then he went away and did his thing. It always helps a detective when he can discuss his case with someone he trusts and make sure he hasn't missed something.'

It paid off. In February 2023, Van Rooyen's teenage nephew, one of her pallbearers, appeared in court charged with her murder.

But commendations fade away in dog-eared albums in a box in Jonathan's kist. And the gaps between calls from former colleagues grow longer and longer. They will never compensate for pens and a braai. They are not medals on his wall. Right now, at the age of 67, only one thing can fill Jonathon's void. And it nearly went down the drain with every glass Aunty Rachel placed on his table.

CHAPTER 18

SELF-CONFESSION

This book is a big deal for Jonathan Morris. It's been on his radar for well over a decade. Back when he was envying medals on colleagues' walls, he was thinking his time would come. 'I knew I would surprise them one day,' he explained when we first started discussing his memoir. 'I've been in many newspapers. But the final chapter would be my book. One day. I think I will be the first detective from Philippi and Mitchells Plain who will have a book out about my investigations. I will be over the moon and back again. It will mean the world to me. I'm a survivor!'

So when his Sizzlers meltdown sent him into a steep nosedive, he must have been disappointed?

We're back to the questions sent over WhatsApp. Jonathan prefers it this way. It gives him time to contemplate the answer. Sometimes that involves a walk from his flat down to the beach, even returning for a nap, before he is ready to reply.

'Jonathan, I've never asked you, what gave you the idea to learn how to use a laptop and start typing your cases? Especially while you were in a terrible mental state?'

It's an obvious question that I'd never got round to asking. And in retrospect, if I had asked it too early, I doubt I'd have got the truth.

'I wrote down most of my cases in longhand in a book and found it difficult when I read it,' he responds. 'There were so many scratchings out. I realised it's gonna take forever. On the other hand, answering your questions on the phone felt like I was under cross-examination in and out of the crime scene.' This is followed by a laughing face emoji. He likes using emojis. 'I decided to take a little crash course in typing with family members. I soon realised it was much easier and I could use the delete button and everything was neat and tidy. I fell in love with the laptop.'

'Before you discovered laptop therapy, did you fear it might be game over for your book? '

'No.'

'Not once?

'You were traumatised and then just started laptopping?'

'Being not able to discuss the crime scene was a setback in carrying on with the book. It was a difficult time, and I experienced flashbacks again of the scene.'

'And that didn't scare you in the slightest, that your book might never appear?'

Jonathan disappears offline. A few hours later he returns, I sense after a long walk.

'I started drinking heavily to cope with the flashbacks.'

Jonathan is no angel. He enjoyed a drink. He chased a dop with his gang unit brothers now and then. But this is the first I hear that he has been medicating with alcohol.

'Truly?'

'Embarrassing truth.' With a shameful-faced emoji.

Following his Sizzlers meltdown, the Confessor Cop went from an occasional drinker to binge-drinking up to two bottles of Scottish Leader a week. His ritual was sharing a bottle once a week at his cousin's place in Grassy Park. At home alone he would klap a bottle once or twice a week, too often in one sitting. The frequency of each binge depended on how many days it took the Confessor Cop to recover.

'So you would leave home to go drinking in Grassy Park? That's a distance of more than 40 kilometres.'

'Yes. I visited my very sick cousin and made it a drinking opportunity. I don't enjoy drinking alone.'

Aunty Rachel would start the ritual, laying out glasses, ice and water neatly on a table in the entertainment room, where Jonathan's bedridden 82-year-old cousin Donald Botha lay. In the background the TV hummed quietly 24/7 on DStv Channel 182, National Geographic.

Donald didn't drink. But Mervin, father-in-law to Donald's daughter, would join the cousins and help Jonathan empty a bottle while they chatted about the old days.

'We would laugh and joke and sometimes argue if we disagreed about stuff from the past. I really enjoyed the wonderful days with Donald and will never forget them. He was a good listener and had a good memory.'

Laughing and reminiscing until the bottle was empty helped Jonathan forget. But it was a slippery slope.

'By the next day I was back to square one.'

Fleeing from his flashbacks. Imagining himself as one of the victims. Being tortured... Being smothered... The horror in that room! Eish!

Back to square one, watching Aunty Rachel set the table again. Then drinking again. To forget his pain. And again. During Donald's dying days.

It was a vicious circle.

'I was watching the dream of my book fall apart knowing that if I didn't pull myself together it was over. Sometimes it felt like I was killing a part of myself while watching Donald slowly dying.'

'How would you get home?'

'My wife is my driver. She would drop me off and go to the Chinese shop and fetch me four hours later. She doesn't drink. She's very religious. She also had family in Grassy Park she could visit.'

'So Leonore watched this for two months before saying anything?'

'She spoke about it and I didn't like the nagging. One day, I was having a drink on my own and she put her foot down and hid the bottle. From then on she would hide a bottle at the end of the evening before I could flatten it. I was too drunk to notice. I then decided to stop my nonsense after a serious lecture and a prayer from her. I did not want to upset my wife as we were both getting old. She was the one who always prayed. She prayed to the Lord that I must slow down on my drinking. I do have her permission if I want to take a drink, but since her intervention the desire is not there.'

'Was this a gradual process to stop drinking?'

'Yes. But I'm done. I still have the half bottle Lenore hid on the shelf. I look at it and we are not friends any more.'

CHAPTER 19

REVELATIONS

WhatsApp is Jonathan's confessional. He feels safe there. Not judged for following Scottish Leader up the garden path. It was a relief, he confessed, to unburden himself. His 'advokaat' apparently was also his moonlighting priest. I wondered if there was more to come.

We returned to the topic of his memoir. It was important, he had explained earlier, because finally people would recognise him for his achievements.

'What did you mean?'

I'm curious to establish if this need for recognition is simply a workplace issue or rooted in his early childhood. He hasn't spoken much of those foundation days. Yet in the criminal cases in this book, he always wanted to find out about the guilty party's background and early life. Jonathan struggles with my question.

'How would you like to be seen by your grandchildren?'

'I want them to see that their grandfather was a hard worker for almost 40 years in the police. That he was a dedicated cop and the medals would have been the proof.'

'Okay, but why are you proud of yourself?'

'Self-praise is no commendation, no medal. It's difficult to praise myself. I don't like bragging about myself.'

After that I didn't expect to hear from him for a while. But a week later his introspection arrives in the form of a Word document titled 'Jonathan describing Jonathan', and a forwarded email from his maternal cousin, Stephanie.

Initially there were no great surprises from Stephanie. But what she said was revealing. Jonathan had asked her to describe him for me, as she and his son-in-law, Elroy Less, were the two family members who showed the most interest in his career.

Stephanie grew up in Durban and only met Jonathan in 1998 when, at the age of 29, she moved to Cape Town with her boyfriend, Russel.

Even so, 'it feels like I've known Jonathan all my life', she wrote in her email. 'Jonathan and his family were always there for me, especially when my son's dad and I split up, leaving me alone with my eight-month-old baby. When he visited he'd put money in my hand as he could see that I was struggling as a single parent.'

Stephanie became intrigued by Jonathan's cases and soon became a sympathetic ear to his personal struggles.

He was 'devoted' to his work but made time for family, especially his mother, explained Stephanie. 'He was very nurturing and always saw that she was provided for. He visited his mother often and she always made sure to have a hot plate of food for him. During those times he was married, but it seemed his wife was not always caring towards him and his children from his previous relationships. His situation improved when he moved back to his mother's home. She provided nutritious meals and ensured his clothes were washed and ironed. She knew that being well dressed was important to Jonathan. Being well presented is part of his character.

'Jonathan was accustomed to a home with good, clean habits and good family values and this formed the basis of his success. This was his stabilising force. Family and a good home base were key to Jonathan's sense of security and peace of mind. He knew that he could go home to these comforts and support structures at his mother's home.'

What puzzled me was that Jonathan had barely mentioned his mother during our discussions. Indeed, why does Stephanie's nurturing, loving matriarch hardly appear in the biographical document he sent me when we started with his memoir?

'We all leaned on that level of nurturing and support that his mother provided,' Stephanie wrote. 'My dear aunt's home in Mitchells Plain was a haven for all of her nine children, her grandchildren, great-grandchildren, extended family, friends and neighbours.

'I'm not exaggerating when I say that many cups of tea and a sandwich was made throughout the day, all day, for whoever popped in. My aunt kept the nicer Jacobs coffee hidden in the cupboard for me when I visited. I loved visiting Jonathan's mom. We were all nurtured there emotionally and with a lovely meal and we didn't even need to do the dishes afterwards. We could sit and chat and enjoy just being nourished.

'Money and supplies for these meals were taken care of by Jonathan. He knew that we all partook and continued to provide even after he moved out, when he married Leonore. He enjoyed that providing was his mother's love language.

'Jonathan became popular with the media, especially when he moved over to the Hawks and was involved in solving high-profile cases. The media became interested in more than just the details of each case but also what Jonathan wore to each court appearance. Brightly coloured ties with a different crisply ironed shirt and a black or brown leather jacket. This was his statement attire. His faded red Toyota Corolla became well known and even made a few television news appearances until he was given a new blue BMW, which caused some controversy with his colleagues.

'What always fascinated me was how Jonathan could get a confession out of a suspect. His secret was gaining their trust in a meaningful way. To this day I still marvel at his ability to do this. Jonathan could see guilt in their eyes and would spend time carefully building a rapport with them, and then the detailed confession would come.

'Jonathan is by no means a saint or perfect. His talent and dedication to his job came at a price. His down-time sometimes included one too many whiskies and his family having to put him safely to bed. He was never rude or rowdy but extra loving and humorous when he had too much to drink. One could never become upset when he was that way but just be amused. The challenge was to ensure that he did not get hurt.

'I was very happy when Jonathan connected with his long-time neighbour who lost her husband. Leonore was married to a pastor and was alone for almost two years before she started dating Jonathan. She is without a doubt the best thing that could happen to him.

'Jonathan's mother felt the same way. She, too, saw Leonore is beautiful inside and out and a kind gentle soul who lets Jonathan shine. As a retired nurse, Leonore makes sure her husband's health comes first. They bring out the best in one another and now live a quiet and fulfilling life together, giving one another what is needed to be content.'

That was the perfect place for Stephanie to end her loving testimonial. But she drops a bomb about an unsolved murder that has haunted Jonathan to this day. Haunted him more than Sizzlers. It was so painful he's never discussed it with any family member. He simply cannot, explained Stephanie.

I'm hoping 'Jonathan describing Jonathan' will speak about it. After all, he has read Stephanie's email. Instead the document confuses me. Is this another family member or a colleague describing Jonathan?

Then slowly, as I run my eye down the list, I realise Jonathan is writing about himself. But in a most unconventional way.

He is a private person.

He loved his work and was a thorough investigating officer.

He is very sensitive and avoids liars and bossy people.

He respects people who respect others and does not appreciate empty promises as he does not make empty promises.

He is a very proud and neat person and likes to dress smart.

He can easily cut people out of his life when insulted and never communicate with them again.

He will not hesitate to defend people and himself when under attack.

He is fearless when it comes to the protection of his family, friends and the community and has been in shooting incidents where he came out on top.

He has a 100% conviction rate in the high court and has been applauded by judges for excellent investigation.

He is a workhorse and when he investigates a new case, he will be the last person to leave the crime scene and will not rest until the case is solved.

He never refused when called out to a crime scene, even if he is not on standby duties; he is willing to assist.

He is a bit of a lone ranger when it comes to searching for information and interviewing informers.

'Jonathan describing Jonathan' is disquieting reading. In over four decades of journalism, I've never encountered anything like it. Has he taken his laptopping too far? Or should I say, has the laptopping taken him too far? Has it merely put a Band-Aid on his PTSD?

I recall reading about sports celebrities referring to themselves in the third person by name. It's known as illeism and could indicate dissociative identity disorder, previously known as split personality disorder or multiple personality disorder. Or schizophrenia. Or borderline personality disorder.

I ask ChatGPT for information, citing a friend who uses illeism, Should I be concerned?

The response is a host of psychological benefits:

'By stepping outside of oneself linguistically, individuals become the observer of their experiences rather than getting overwhelmed by them. They gain a clearer understanding of their thoughts, feelings and behaviours. This self-distancing from their negative inner monologue allows individuals to adopt more self-compassion. This enhances self-esteem and well-being. Some studies have found that illeism can also shift focus and attention away from dysregulating emotions to tasks at hand.'

These benefits are why sportsmen deploy illeism. Some swear by it. Like retired ultra-endurance athlete Christopher Bergland, who used illeism to break records and continues to write about and promote the tool.

Jonathan seems to be in healthy company. No matter how creepy it sounds, referring to yourself in the third person can be functional.

Cognitive behavioural therapy, eye-movement desensitisation and reprocessing therapy, and narrative therapy all use linguistic techniques, including illeism, to treat trauma. Psychotherapist Kim Schneiderman, author of *Step Out Of Your Story*, promotes narrative therapy where participants reframe their traumatic experiences and memories with third-person stories and writing exercises that transform their lives.

'Every life is an unfolding story,' she writes, 'a dynamic, unique, purposeful, and potentially heroic story with bright spots, turning points, and abounding opportunities for personal growth and transformation. From the day we're born, we become the star and spin doctor of our own work in progress, with the power to tell our stories as triumphs, tragedies, or something in between.'

Spin doctoring in the third person, she explains, tricks your protective, censoring ego into thinking you're writing about somebody else. The process promotes a sense of self-liberation and self-compassion. Literally you become less attached to your trauma.

Unwittingly, Jonathan has been doing something similar on his laptop. As he types away, the freaked-out detective on the Sizzlers scene has unconsciously coached himself to become more the neutral witness of the drama.

However, Jonathan claims he simply wrote 'Jonathan describing Jonathan' so it wouldn't sound like he was boasting. 'I felt I can better describe myself,' he says. 'It's the first time I've ever done this.'

Nevertheless, the intuitive way he compiled 'Jonathan describing Jonathan' suggests he has been practising third-person self-talk unconsciously for longer than he admits.

Are there other ways that Jonathan is surreptitiously maintaining emotional equilibrium? Could the rhythm of his typing in the still, early hours be tapping his vagal nerve, for example?

According to polyvagal theory, the ventral vagal network, which runs from the diaphragm to the brain stem, forming part of the parasympathetic nervous system, plays a crucial role in regulating our physiological responses to stress and trauma. Deep breathing and meditation can sync that network. So, too, can seemingly innocuous, repetitive sounds like humming, chanting, toning and singing. Even vigorous gargling can be healing.

A leading polyvagal theory proponent, Peter Levine, suggests gently growling like an animal on your exhale during rhythmic breathing can calm the body and mind. And it may prompt laughter, which, as we all know, is the best medicine.

But Jonathan doesn't make a sound while he types. All you hear is his tapping of the keyboard.

'Oh yes. And loud too. I'm Mr One-Finger!'

I then ask ChatGPT about keyboard tapping and polyvagal theory.

'There's no research evidence that it regulates the vagal network. However, it's plausible that laptop keyboard tapping, especially when paired with a sense of focus or enjoyment, could contribute to calming the nervous system.'

It all makes sense. Laptop therapy has clearly generated healing consequences that enabled Jonathan to return to his crime scenes and document them without relapse. But there's a loose end. What about the gruesome Sizzlers crime scene photos in a lever-arch file in a kist at the bottom of Jonathan's bed? Since he told me this bizarre detail, I've never been able to make sense of it. If Sizzlers torments him, why sleep with these photographs nearby?

'Looking at the photos makes me feel proud of myself. It was the biggest case I've solved in my whole career. They are the medals I never received.'

They remind him of the suffering of 'his boys'.

He owes it to 'his boys', he says, to make sure they are seen at Woest's next parole hearing. 'One look at those photos will tell them what sort of killer they are considering releasing. I had a lot of interaction with Woest and I'm convinced that he will kill again if released.'

But there are deeper reasons why Jonathan holds the photos close.

'They could be a way for the detective to process his feelings and emotions surrounding the traumatic event,' explains ChatGPT. 'It's possible that the detective has not fully come to terms with the impact of the case on his mental and emotional well-being. The detective may find some form of solace or closure in periodically revisiting the photos, even though they evoke painful memories. It's important to note that everyone copes with trauma differently. What may seem unusual or disturbing to one person may be a meaningful, necessary coping mechanism for another.'

CHAPTER 20

EPIPHANIES

There is a backstory to Jonathan Morris that comes out bit by bit during our WhatsApp interviews. Stories like this one from the late 1970s at the Hanover Park bus terminus.

Jonathan's got a gangster called Doctor Mongrel by the throat and he's squeezing hard, bringing tears to the man's eyes. But it's Jonathan's 7.65mm pressed into his crudely tattooed neck that's got the full attention of the Mongrels leader. The safety's off, there's a round in the chamber, the 21-year-old detective constable means business.

Earlier, he had sent warning to the Doctor not to plan robberies in plain sight on his watch. But instead of listening, the gangster decided to intimidate the rookie by getting in his face with six of his 'soldiers' circling.

'Call off your dogs now,' says Jonathan. 'Or you will die where you stand!'

By now the Doctor's round spectacles, as thick as Coke bottles, have slipped far enough down his long nose and Jonathan can see fear in his gerookte eyes. The man is stoned. He is also quivering. All about them are people standing dead still, stunned fruit sellers and pedestrians ready to dive for cover.

'Ouens, staan terug!' shouts the Doctor. [Guys, move off.]

Today he's afraid, this man who habitually terrorises the terminus and Johndown Walk.

'Dis okay, ouens!'

Jonathan catches a whiff of urine, pungent. The Mongrels retreat. He releases the Doctor. Then hits him across the back of the head and literally kicks his wet arse.

'Fokkof, jou gemors! Voertsek!'

Of this encounter, Jonathan says, 'I do not want to paint myself as an angel in the police. If Doctor Mongrel hadn't called off his dogs I would've had to pull the trigger where he stood. If I didn't, I was a dead man.' That could have ended Jonathan's career there and then.

At about the same time a movie called *Dirty Harry*, starring Clint Eastwood as a cop, was showing. In it the Eastwood cop, Dirty Harry, has a gangster in a similar position to Jonathan and the Doctor. The first time this scene occurs, the gangster gets out alive. The second time, he doesn't.

Jonathan warmed to this analogy with Dirty Harry. He feels his actions came out of sheer frustration. The Mongrels were notorious for robbing people at the bus terminus, which was in SAP's Philippi precinct where Jonathan was stationed for the first five years of his police career. Hanover Park Lounge & Bar, the adjacent bottle store and the suburb's main street, Johndown Walk, were the gang's scavenging grounds. Any resistance was dealt with ruthlessly.

'The Mongrels were evil. They liked to rob pensioners and wouldn't hesitate to stab anyone who resisted.'

By his third year at Philippi, Jonathan had had enough. In short, he was gatvol of the never-ending daily robberies. So when Doctor Mongrel ignored his warning and interrupted his search for suspects at the terminus, the rookie detective played Dirty Harry.

Six months later the two crossed paths again, this time at the opening of Hanover Park swimming pool. Jonathan and his colleagues were mingling with the excited crowd, shooing away every Mongrel they could find, when the Doctor made another stupid error of judgment.

'Wie is jy om my manskappe weg te jaag van die pool af?' he demanded, wagging his finger in Jonathan's face. [Who are you to chase away my men?]

Again Jonathan reacted angrily.

'My first blow was right between his eyes. I hit him so hard I split his glasses in two and dropped him where he stood.' He then kicked the squirming gangster until his colleagues dragged him away.

'I was befok angry. I could have killed him that day.'

The gangster slunk off ... to the police station, where he laid an assault charge against Jonathan.

It went nowhere.

'I fought almost every day and weekends with the Mongrels. The gangsters laid many assault charges against me. But they were all withdrawn. I was gatvol of them by the time I left Philippi, but they never broke my spirit. I learnt very early in my career not to show any weakness. I was from the community so I was streetwise. I knew their language. I learnt the hard way that you have to be hard, even violent, to earn their respect.'

This didn't just apply to gangsters.

'I remember when I attended domestic violence complaints there were times the perpetrator would disrespect me. I took no nonsense. I would smack him down to the ground and make sure that he will not lift his hand to his wife again. The complainants never wanted to lay criminal charges so I took the law into my own hands. I had to. I couldn't just walk away. The same with suspects who resisted arrest. I had to use physical force to fulfil my daily task. I had to send a message to the community who were watching that Morris took no kak.'

And then there's a story from even earlier in his life.

'It was the worst time of my school career.' He was in Standard 6 at Silverstream High in Manenberg. 'I was robbed on a weekly basis by two Born Free Kids gangsters, Greg and Goggie.'

Curiously he had deleted this story from his biography document. He doesn't know why. Perhaps it was simply the fear of revealing his shadow side in public.

'Greg and Goggie threatened me with knives for my two cents bus fare almost every day.'

Besides being armed, the gangsters were in their late twenties.

'Fighting them was out of the question. So I changed my route to the bus stop. But they always managed to intercept me. By the end of Standard 6, I was so traumatised that I almost failed. I told my mom that if she didn't find another school I was quitting school. I refused point-blank to go back to Silverstream.'

Jonathan's mother managed to organise a place in Standard 7 at Oaklands High.

'It was such a relief to catch the bus without being bullied,' says Jonathan. 'I was happy again.'

Then one Saturday afternoon, while waiting for a bus, he spotted Greg riding his bicycle in Lansdowne Road. Jonathan was now 13.

'My heart was racing and my mouth went dry when he rode right up to me and asked where he could buy dagga. I said I didn't know and as he rode off, I realised he hadn't recognised me.'

Thinking the gangster might return the way he came, Jonathan armed himself with a brick and a wooden baton he found on the pavement.

'For self-protection?'

'Revenge, my brother. Revenge.'

Five minutes later, Jonathan's wish was fulfilled. Throwing the brick squarely at Greg's chest, he sent him flying.

'Jy, whitey, jou ma se poes, wat maak jy?' whimpered Greg. [You whitey, you cunt, what are you doing?]

Unleashing more pent-up anger, Jonathan beat the baton across Greg's head and back. Then he smashed his bicycle. Greg fled, threatening retaliation that never materialised. And Jonathan was happy.

'I knew then why they say revenge is sweet.'

Jonathan also had the last laugh with Goggie. During his first year as a cop, who should arrive in prison overalls to clean Philippi Police Station but Goggie!

'I asked him if he remembered robbing me. He said he couldn't but he apologised. I told him that I forgave him. He's lucky he ran into me when he did. If it was before I became a cop, I would have fucked him up the same as Greg.'

While the school-going Jonathan was no longer being terrorised, his marks were down and he failed Standard 8. 'Maybe I was dom. Just stupid.' The way he says it, you can hear the self-criticism.

Jonathan passed his repeat year but then had to drop out at 16 for 'personal reasons' to become an admin clerk at Murray & Stewart's building construction office in Philippi.

'I had to find a job because my mother was struggling to make ends meet,' he reluctantly admits later, during one of our sessions that was tantamount to a cross-examination.

In his biography document, he is sketchy about this life changer, as he is about most of his formative first 18 years. Intriguingly, there is hardly any reference to his mother.

Another glaring omission from his early years is his first love, whom he meets during his second working year. He was about to turn 18. Only much laptopping later are the painful reasons revealed.

He was open, however, about the big career game changer of 1976 which happened during a Christmas lunch at his neighbour's house. There he met a young police constable.

By then Jonathan and his mates were big fans of Springbok Radio's 'Squad Cars', one of the most popular weekly series broadcast on South African radio.

Each show was a dramatised version of a real police case that ended with an addictive 'listen again' message that hooked many a teenage boy:

'They prowl the empty streets at night. Waiting. In fast cars, on foot. Living with crime and violence. These men are on duty 24 hours out of every 24. They face dangers at every turn, expecting nothing less. They protect the people of South Africa. These are the men of Squad Cars!'

These 30 minutes of captivating Friday-night radio soon had Jonathan and his crew prowling their neighbourhood streets most weekends in the white VW Beetle of his friend Kobus, even managing to foil a few burglaries along the way. When Philippi police

Constable Keyser Titus heard about this over roast chicken that Christmas, he encouraged Jonathan to sign up to the police force.

At first Jonathan was cautious, schooled by his mother's concern whenever the Springboks lost a rugby match. 'Die polisie is kwaad en slaan almal wat hulle in die straat sien,' she would tell him.

'We believed her and it was confirmed after neighbourhood friends were assaulted by the cops after the Springboks lost a rugby match. Personally I never had an altercation with a policeman because I kept my distance. But the cops I saw looked scary, rough and ready to stop-and-search and send you on your way with a smack and a kick up the arse. So like all the kids on the farm where we lived, I would automatically run away as soon as I saw a police van approaching.'

But Keyser was different.

'He was the first policeman I spoke to and wasn't scary at all. He was friendly and treated me with respect. He was a real gentleman towards me and took a genuine interest in my crime-fighting efforts.'

There was another lesson here: not to see everyone as the same. Keyser was a cop but he was also kind. There was something here that Jonathan would later integrate into his interviewing technique.

This Christmas lunch with the policeman also shifted Jonathan's vision of his own life.

'I was enjoying my first job at Murray & Stewart. I was well liked by my colleagues and was given responsibilities above my admin clerk pay grade. I knew I had a career there. But after meeting Keyser, my life purpose suddenly became as clear as daylight. I wanted to serve and protect the community like those Squad Cars cops.'

Jonathan admits that his decision was socially and politically controversial.

Six months earlier, police had gunned down peacefully demonstrating students during the 16 June 1976 'Soweto Uprising'. By August, the unrest had spread to Cape Town's townships, where black and coloured students marched in solidarity, torching schools, libraries and courts and clashing violently with police.

In September the following year, the Black Consciousness activist Steve Biko died in detention after having been tortured. He was the 20th person to die in police custody in 18 months. A month later the white minority government banned 18 anti-apartheid political organisations, most of them allied to the Black Consciousness Movement, detained scores of activists, and gagged the media.

As an 18-year-old, Jonathan, however, was an apolitical breadwinner battling to make ends meet for his mother and six siblings.

'What happened during the riots did not affect me at all because, to tell you the truth, I had no interest or clue why there was fighting between the blacks and the whites. I just accepted the conditions we lived under. There were no activists in Philippi raising political awareness. I saw policemen shooting at the coloureds who were stoning cars and for me it seemed normal because it was wrong to stone cars. I was a law-abiding citizen.' And he had his heart set on being a policeman.

Keyser helped Jonathan fill in his application forms and by April 1977, three months before his 19th birthday, the student constable was taking witness statements in the Philippi charge office for R92 a month.

Keyser taught him the ropes and Jonathan was inspired to be like him.

'He set a good example of what a policeman should be. He was strict but respectful, no matter who you were. He did his job without fear or favour. I learnt a lot from him.'

Just like Keyser, Jonathan took pride in shining his shoes and ironing his uniform every morning – even though it was khaki for coloureds and blacks, not the blue reserved for whites only. Even though the K in his force number K165869N stood for 'kleurling'. Coloured. Even though a white warrant officer could, without asking and while looking him in the eye, remove 50 cents from his monthly pay-packet for an unknown white brigadier's retirement gift. Even though coloureds carried old Smith & Wesson revolvers and six bullets each that they had to check in before knocking off.

While white colleagues carried 9mm parabellums that they did not have to hand in before leaving for the day. And they stored a shotgun and an R1 rifle at home.

There was no doubt that the apartheid state regarded Jonathan as a second-class cop. The indignity was a crime against his humanity. But politics couldn't contain his passion. That's how badly he wanted to be a detective. A first-class one.

CHAPTER 21

SKOP, SKIET EN DONNER

For Jonathan, the trauma of being a policeman started just a few months into the job. He was on night shift, booking out firearms. When Constable Valentine received his revolver from Jonathan, he loaded it in silence, raised it to the rookie's head and said, 'Vanaand skiet ek jou vrek!' [Tonight I'm going to shoot you dead.]

Jonathan could smell booze on Valentine's breath. Caught between disbelief and visceral fear, he held his breath until Valentine turned and left without another word.

'Constables liked to bully students,' explains Jonathan. 'But from the start I stood up for myself and never allowed it. Some of them, like Valentine, did not enjoy that I was hardegat. But I never imagined any of them would react like he did.'

When Valentine returned to the charge office hours later with two arrested suspects, he behaved as if he hadn't threatened Jonathan earlier. Chalking it up as a one-off, Jonathan helped Valentine lock away his suspects. But instead of leaving, Valentine joined the rookie in his nightshift headcount of those in the cells. Everything went smoothly until they entered the juvenile cell. Recognising a sleeping youngster, Valentine suddenly began kicking him awake. Then, without warning, he shouted, 'Ek ken jou, jy is 'n ou skelm.' [I know you, you're a villain.] With that, he drew his revolver and shot him in the head.

Jonathan ran to the charge office to report the incident and call an ambulance. The victim was rushed to hospital and miraculously survived emergency surgery.

'It was the first time I saw a person being shot. It traumatised me. I could've taken that bullet to the head.'

Valentine was suspended and gave Jonathan his first taste of court, where his testimony put his colleague behind bars for attempted murder, albeit for only 18 months.

After that incident, and for the first six months of 1978, while he was at Bishop Lavis Training College, the closest he came to a violent incident was when his sadistic law instructor tried to discipline him.

'Sergeant September enjoyed hitting us across our fingers with a ruler. The day he came to me, I looked him in the eye and refused to put my hands out. He left me alone after that. College made a man out of me,' reflects Jonathan. 'By the time I turned 20, I'd learnt how to iron my clothes and be self-disciplined. Most of my instructors respected me and I was ready to serve.'

Halfway through college, Jonathan became a father to a son. Then four months later, three days after his 20th birthday, his second son was born.

These important personal details Jonathan doesn't tell me directly. Up to this point I was aware that he had two sons born to different mothers. But only when I asked for his sons' birth dates did I see that they were conceived within months of each other with women he hadn't named. He also didn't care to discuss the experience.

'I don't want to go there. It's not something to be proud of.'

The responsibility made him even more determined to be a good cop. By the end of 1978, after six months on the beat in Wetton, he knew he wanted to be a career detective.

'I got tired of the beat. It was boring. And the rules started to get to me. I was good enough to look after white people's houses but prohibited from arresting a white suspect. Jy kan nie die baas toesluit nie. [You can't lock up the boss.] Investigation excited me. The community respected detectives. The guys with the brains who go the extra mile to solve a case, those were the cops who were feared. I wanted to be a detective who criminals feared.'

Becoming one, though, carried a price.

Before hanging up his uniform, Jonathan experienced his first murder scene. The victim was called Liefling from the Laughing Boy Kids. His head had been diced by panga-wielding Mongrels. 'I could see his brains. What a traumatic sight. I was also scared because I knew it would be the first of many murder scenes.'

Bullets also started flying once Jonathan became a detective constable at Philippi.

One morning, while trying to arrest a bicycle thief in Lansdowne Road opposite Nyanga, the suspect pulled a knife. Jonathan's warrant officer partner stopped the thief in his tracks. 'Dead. One shot. Right in front of me. No questions asked. It was the first time I experienced a person being shot dead. I was shocked for weeks.'

This is what kept Jonathan's trauma time-bomb ticking. One violent death after another. For four decades.

During that career, Jonathan was only fired at twice. The first time was at the age of 23 while chasing car thieves across a dark Hanover Park field.

'They turned and the next thing I heard bullets flying around me. It made me realise that this wasn't a movie. I could die every day I came on duty. Just like that.'

Amazingly, Jonathan only pulled the trigger three times in his four decades. Two of those occasions were while stationed at Philippi. It made him feel less helpless. But it added to his trauma.

One Friday afternoon in 1980, he received a tip that an armed robbery suspect, Keith Constance aka Katokkie, was hiding out in an Athlone flat. Because it was off his precinct, he sought backup from Athlone detectives. But they were too busy braaiing.

So Jonathan and partner Constable Karel Noemdo, guns drawn, kicked down the door themselves and found three men partying. Jonathan blocked Katokkie as he made a dash for one of the rooms. With the angry crowd outside baying, 'Wat maak die boere hier?' [What are the cops doing here?], Jonathan knew his arrest had to be snappy.

Outside, Katokkie took advantage of the pressing crowd and

broke free from the other two suspects. Cool as Dirty Harry, Walther PP 7.65 still in hand, Jonathan raised his right arm and fired before Katokkie could round the corner.

'I hit him in his backside and sent him sliding across the ground on his arse. In that moment I felt invincible.'

But Jonathan sobered in an instant. The crowd were riotous. He and Noemdo had to get out quickly.

Later Jonathan returned to the scene with Athlone backup. In the room that Katokkie had run towards, they found a fully loaded Taurus .38 Special and a box of bullets. 'Katokkie was going for his gun. If I hadn't stopped him, it would've been a different ball game. I would've had to send him to his ancestors.'

It was chilling lesson for the young cop, who later heard that Katokkie was arrested by Murder and Robbery detectives for several armed robbery cases. 'Sometimes, in the height of an arrest, it can feel like you're playing cops-and-robbers. But being windgat can get you killed. Every time I kicked down a door after that it was with a humble head.'

Jonathan pulled the trigger a second time late one Saturday night in 1981 after leaving a friend's Hanover Park house. A married couple, who recognised him, said their nearby flat was being ransacked by a Mongrels trio. Two escaped as Jonathan entered the flat, pistol in hand, but he managed to nab Ougat Mongrel, a feared youngster easily recognised by the word GOD tattooed across his forehead.

On the way back to his cop car, a green Chev, some Mongrel reinforcements distracted Jonathan long enough for Ougat to make a break. Without skipping a beat, the detective constable dropped Ougat with one round to his leg.

'I always aimed for a fleeing suspect's legs because my life was not in danger. But if my life was under threat, I wouldn't hesitate to shoot to kill.'

Not for the first time in our conversations, I wondered if this rule of thumb applied to Jonathan protecting his family. Was he capable of resurrecting the ruthlessness he displayed at 13, this time with a service pistol in hand?

The never-ending confrontations with Mongrels and other gangs were a constant source of stress for the rookie detective. Not only was each run-in a threat to life and limb, they easily triggered Jonathan's Dirty Harry streak, which always carried the potential to wreck his career.

To make matters worse, the gangsters had an unlikely ally in the Philippi detective commander. He grew weary of having to deal with the endless stream of flimsy assault charges they laid against Jonathan. Instead of accepting the admin that came with the territory, the commander made it personal. Jonathan also noticed there was more to being singled out. When Philippi's white detectives assaulted suspects in their offices, the commander turned a blind eye. 'I also caught him once assaulting a black detective sergeant who was old enough to be his father. The commander wasn't much older than me. I found it hard to respect him after that. I also got the sense that he would have liked to smack me around, but he knew I wouldn't take it lying down.'

Instead the commander chose the passive-aggressive route.

'Gaan doen die donnerse ondersoek nou,' he would write in Jonathan's investigation dockets. [Go and do the bloody investigation now.] 'Die fokken ondersoek sal gedoen word,' Jonathan's pen would fire back. [The fucking work will be done.]

And so it went on until eventually Jonathan's Dirty Harry got the better of him. And made the commander's day.

One Saturday evening shortly before Christmas 1980, Jonathan raced to the assistance of a reservist being attacked inside Hanover Lounge. There he found Constable Shericke stumbling around bleeding after having been knifed in the neck.

'Hulle moet jou vrek gesteek het,' yelled a gangster in the gathering hysterical crowd. [They should have knifed you dead.] Jonathan snapped and let rip with his baton, dropping the gangster. As the crowd scattered, Jonathan's partner, Detective Constable September, put his boot in for good measure.

Forced to cut short his Mossel Bay Christmas holiday to investigate the discipline breach of his men, the commander was furious.

'He told me that this time he'd make sure I go to jail.'

Both detectives were later found guilty of assault with intent to do grievous bodily harm and sentenced to a R30 fine or six months' imprisonment plus six months suspended for five years. The commander looked like the cat who got the cream. And ready to pounce again once word spread and delighted gangland began taunting Jonathan.

Scared of going to jail, Jonathan tried to restrain his Dirty Harry. 'I tried to walk away when provoked and call for backup instead of meeting fire with fire.'

But old habits die hard.

Several weeks after his court humiliation, a Mongrel suspect deliberately yanked Jonathan's tie during an interrogation. 'He laughed, saying I could do nothing because I was suspended. He was wrong. I knocked him to the ground and dragged him scream-ing past the commander's office to the cells.'

The gangster's assault charge fell flat because two colleagues monitoring Jonathan's interrogation vouched for him. But deep down, Jonathan knew this wasn't the way to behave. 'I was skating on thin ice.'

Ironically, five Mongrels helped Jonathan change his ways. While arresting them at their Johndown Walk hideout for the fatal stab-bing of a schoolboy, two of the gangsters resisted until subdued by Jonathan's baton. On the way back to the station, when they tried to kick open the doors of his Chev, he beat them about the legs.

Lead investigator Detective Sergeant Jan Thorne was apoplectic when he heard how his suspects had been assaulted. But he didn't do as the commander had. Instead the veteran, who was like a father to Philippi's rookie detectives, pulled Jonathan aside and quietly explained, 'You never assault or threaten a murder suspect under any circumstances.'

Patiently Thorne explained how, in his experience, it always caused serious problems for the state in court. In some cases it had led to acquittals, which were unacceptable for any detective worth his salt.

Thorne's wise counsel landed squarely. As did his kindness and respect, which made such an impression on Jonathan that they would replace his baton in his arsenal of law enforcement techniques.

'I knew all of this intellectually but after that discussion I bought into it fully. There was absolutely nothing to gain from assaulting a suspect. If I carried on that way I'd be letting myself down, my badge and the families of victims. The only way forward was to play it by the book if I was serious about becoming the best murder investigator I could possibly be.'

Jonathan's second Philippi epiphany arose from another unexpected source.

A year before he was transferred to Mitchells Plain, he was sent to arrest a murder suspect and was in court when the judge sentenced the man to death. Jonathan knew the sentence was inevitable but still it upset him. Jonathan and a colleague, Detective Sergeant Stanley Lawrence, drove the condemned man back to Pollsmoor. Before leaving the court, the man asked Jonathan to buy him a pie.

'He thanked me with a soft voice.' Jonathan can remember the incident but not the man's name.

On the way to Pollsmoor, Jonathan watched the man quietly eat his pie. 'He looked so humble, sad and confused,' wrote Jonathan at the height of his laptopping. 'We didn't talk. I was just watching him closely in case he tried to jump out of the car. Then I realised that I was watching the last pie this man would ever eat. As I watched, I was overcome by this overwhelming sadness. As I'm typing this I can still feel that intense sadness after all these years.'

At Pollsmoor, the reception was packed with awaiting-trial prisoners. Lawrence handed the conviction papers to a white prison warden who bellowed, 'Staan daardie kant, want jy is ge-condemned.' [Stand that side, because you are condemned.] It was a harsh reality check. 'It didn't make sense, but in that moment I felt guilty for being his arresting officer.'

Later Jonathan would recognise that his flood of empathy was his greatest gift. 'I now know this is the reason I can relate with murderers and get confessions out of them. I think they get comfortable and feel free to talk to me, as I treat them with respect and never make empty promises. What you see is what you get. I rest my case.'

It took a while but for the remainder of his time at Philippi, Jonathan gradually learnt to walk away when provoked and call for backup if necessary. Finally, in 1981, he retired his Dirty Harry when he was transferred to a satellite detective branch at Waterfall Close in Mitchells Plain's Westridge suburb. There was nothing glamorous about his new office located in a converted three-bedroom flat he shared with 10 other detectives from greater Cape Town police stations. With no telephones, they had to make do with two-way radios and between them they shared one old unmarked beige bakkie.

'There were no more gang fights or Mongrels to provoke me every day. I was working with colleagues who respected each other. We respected the community and they respected us and together with excellent reservists we fought crime together. Gone were the days of skop, skiet en donner.'

The makeshift branch was the perfect incubator for Jonathan's newfound sensibility. 'I gradually developed my skills and turned interrogation into a questioning technique that involved respecting the suspect at all times.'

His results spoke for themselves. By the end of 1983, six months after moving into fully equipped offices in Mitchells Plain's new First Avenue Police Station, he nailed his first confession. A confession that withstood four days of exhaustive cross-examination in court. The murderer and rapist of an elderly woman was sent down for 32 years and the Confessor Cop was born.

But although Jonathan was well clear of Philippi by that time, Philippi wasn't done with him.

In those days there was no such thing as an officially traumatised cop, let alone mandated counselling. 'Senior officers taught us that cowboys don't cry. We would discuss our traumatic experiences with a lot of alcohol. That was our trauma counselling. It took four decades for me to see this cowboy suffered in silence for far too long. I should've started laptop therapy a long time ago.'

CHAPTER 22

REDEMPTION

When Jonathan told me the story about Doctor Mongrel, he also said, 'I was determined that no criminal, especially a gang member, would ever dominate me.'

These never-say-never words rang in my ears as I read cousin Stephanie's email, which segues from testimonial into revelation. 'Family means a lot to Jonathan,' Stephanie wrote. 'His mother engrained that in us. He can't handle seeing his family hurt or in trouble. So when he got the news of his son being gunned down by gangsters...'

I struggle to comprehend her words.

'...he was not able to bring himself to visit the scene.'

I thought I pretty much knew everything there was to know about the violence in Jonathan's life. Much of our time had been spent reviewing his many cases and the accompanying violence. Of course, I expected a few surprises. But being a victim of the type of crime he spent his life investigating was not one of them. Nor was the irony that he was one of those many victims left dangling when the case went cold.

'I always asked Jonathan lots of questions about his cases,' explained Stephanie. 'But to this day I have not asked him about *that case*. This one is too close to home and too painful for him to speak about.'

For the first time in my probing of Jonathan's past, I'm clueless about how to proceed. Obviously this has to be part of Jonathan's book. But that means approaching his trauma all over again.

Although Jonathan had forwarded Stephanie's email to me, he

had chosen to remain silent about its content. This amplified my hesitancy. When I broach the subject, Jonathan admits he intended to tell me this story. He just didn't know how. It happened more than a decade ago but he still cannot find the words to describe it.

During a WhatsApp call I hesitantly suggest lapttoping to find the words. Again Jonathan listened so quietly that I thought he had disconnected. Then he said, okay. And the line went dead.

Unexpectedly, a week later a document named, 'Clifford Brandon Lawrence' dropped into my mailbox.

'He was born on 24/07/1978 at Browns Farm, Philippi. Due to personal reasons, me and his mother split and she got married and moved to Rocklands in Mitchells Plain. I was always behind the scenes in his upbringing and he became a fine young gentleman. He had a close relationship with his brother and sisters and was very protective.

'Three years prior to his death it was brought to my attention that he was struggling with drug addiction. It broke my heart. We had many meetings and he went to a couple of drug rehabs and recovered. But after a few months he would relapse and go back again. We fought a losing battle because he did not get any better.'

On Saturday, 23 June 2012, a mere month before Jonathan's 54th birthday, his son-in-law called. Jonathan distinctly recalls the time: 8pm. Here is his account:

It was Elroy. He was wailing. 'Daddy, Daddy, please come to Mitchells Plain. Cliffie has been shot.'

Elroy said that he was on his way to the crime scene. A few minutes later I received a second call from him that my son is deceased and he cried. I went into shock and sat in the lounge in my flat in Kenilworth. I remember I was watching TV alone. Leonore was working night shift looking after a frail patient at a retirement village in Rondebosch.

I just sat in the lounge. I could not get myself to go to the crime scene. I was heartbroken and a thousand thoughts went through my mind.

I imagined how my son is lying in a pool of blood for hours waiting for crime scene investigators and the ballistic unit. People crying and sympathising with me, something I do not take very well. At moments like these I prefer to mourn or suffer in silence.

I did not inform Leonore, because she and my son had a very good relationship. Suddenly I heard a key in the door and Leonore was crying and I realised it was 8.00 in the morning.

I calmed her down and asked her not to cry because I needed her to be strong and support me through this trauma. I needed to get my head clean.

After receiving many phone calls from my family, friends and colleagues I decided to switch my phone off. I was also informed that my mother forced my brother to take her to the crime scene, where she stayed for hours until they removed Cliffie's body.

I have been to hundreds of crime scenes but never in my wildest dreams thought that the day will come that my dead son would be part of a crime scene and that I would not be able to attend it.

I was filled with sadness but somehow there was also calmness in my heart knowing how he struggled with drug addiction. He is no more roaming the streets begging for drug money from family and friends to fill his needs. At least I know where he is.

We had a family gathering the Sunday afternoon and discussed the way forward and made funeral arrangements. On Monday, I applied for a week's leave and was told that the case would not be investigated by our unit, as it was too close to home.

The funeral was on 28/06/2012 (five days later that week) at the Tabernacle of Life Full Gospel Church of God in Rocklands. I was supported by members of our unit, family and friends, Advocate Shareen Riley and colleagues from the NPA. My son was buried at Muizenberg Cemetery.

After a week I was informed that a suspect was arrested with a firearm for questioning in the murder case M/Plain case 1916/06/2012. But the firearm was not linked to the murder.

I received a lot of unreliable information from gang members who blamed the School Boys and the Americans for the shooting at the shebeen. I've never had the courage to visit the crime scene since the shooting. I heard through the grapevine that the case went cold. I was never informed by an investigating officer whoever he might be.

I can indeed relate with victims' families who never got justice for their loved ones, because I am one of them. Who knows, maybe one day a cop will inform us that they solved a cold case and give us closure. Until then we will just hope and wish that it will happen before we close our eyes.

Jonathan is vague about the details around Cliffie's murder. For good reason. He had never seen the docket or spoken to the investigating officer. But from colleagues he learnt that Cliffie was in the vicinity of a Nice Time Kids drughouse in Rocklands, presumably to buy drugs, when it came under attack. There was no hard evidence but word on the ground was that the shooters were Americans or Schoolboys.

In the aftermath, Jonathan was torn between two selves. The Confessor Cop who desired this confession more than any other in his career. And the grief-stricken father, afraid that this trauma would undo him.

'Even now I do not want to see the docket. Because my fear is then I would see Cliffie's post-mortem photos.'

As much as laptop therapy had helped him explore difficult emotions and dark places, Jonathan was scared and ashamed to voice this dark place for the first time.

'When the book is published people might see me as a weak cop who couldn't solve my son's case.'

His rational self knew this made no sense. His Hawks unit superiors would never have allowed him close to the investigation. In fact, mindful of potential retaliation by Jonathan's colleagues, they had handed the case to detectives from another police station.

'Staying away from my son's scene was actually a blessing in disguise,' Jonathan laptops early one morning after our Cliffie conversations. 'If I had shown interest in the case, different gangsters would have whispered their agendas in my ear, hoping to mislead me. That could have ended in tears. I had a very real fear of what would happen if I came face to face with the perpetrators. It could be Doctor Mongrel all over again. Except this time I might have pulled the trigger. You just never know.'

Jonathan's WhatsApp profile has this verse from Isiah: 'No weapon formed against me shall prosper.' It reminds him daily that the consequences for Cliffie's murder were in God's hands, not in his own vengeful thoughts. He truly believes that, while realising that it is human to err.

'I have never approached a crime scene with hate and revenge. There were times that the thought came to my mind that certain killers don't deserve to live. But by the time I came to questioning a murderer, I could see he was a human being like you or me.

To be honest, I still don't know how I would react if I was tipped off about the identity of Cliffie's killer. It would be new territory for me. The bottom line is that Cliffie's killer or killers hurt me and my family in the cruellest way. And no matter what, you must never touch my family.'

It was inevitable that Jonathan's pain would be magnified by his last conversation with Cliffie, which had happened two weeks before, at his daughter's Rocklands home. Simone, his second eldest daughter from his first marriage, and Cliffie were close.

'I remember his hair was long and he was dirty. I gave him money to go cut his hair and clean himself. He promised me that he would come back and I must wait for him. It got late and I thought that maybe he had used the money for drugs and wasn't coming back. So I left. The next day Simone told me Cliffie had returned and looked so beautiful. How I wish I could have waited just a little longer to see my boy.'

Leonore was Jonathan's saving grace.

The couple had been living together for two years and were four months away from their long-planned wedding when Cliffie was shot. Leonore insisted they should postpone. But amid the agony and bewilderment Jonathan realised it would be another form of loss that would multiply his sadness.

'I needed her by my side to get through the grief. She is a God-fearing woman who spiritually supports me. She constantly prays for me. And that helped me cope.'

Jonathan avoided therapy and leaning on family or friends for sympathy. Leonore's consoling, learnt from years of nursing experience, was sufficient.

'I don't take sympathy very well. I get emotional and become scared that I will cry in front of people. And remember, cowboys don't cry. I cry when I'm alone and in front of my wife. She consoled lots of patients and families who lost loved ones. She just knows how to handle my situation.'

Jonathan is yet to find the same grace with Clifford's mother, whom he names for the first time while discussing Cliffie. But only after being asked.

'I met my son Clifford's mom in 1976,' he WhatsApps. 'And in 1978 we broke up because she had an affair with a close friend of mine. She got married in the early-1980s. After my son's death we never spoke about the incident. We only discussed the funeral arrangements. She also mentioned that she forgave the unknown perpetrators in a newspaper interview. I saw her in January 2024 at her brother-in-law's funeral. We greeted but never spoke about my late son.'

Sometimes fewer words speak louder than a plethora of details. They are enough for me to work out that the breakup occurred when Cliffie was no more than six months old. Jonathan doesn't say so directly, but several hearts were broken while he was experiencing his baptism of fire as a teenage cop.

He coped by leapfrogging into another relationship, getting married shortly before Christmas 1979.

I learned something more about him during our Cliffie conversations. In 2014, two years after Cliffie was shot, Jonathan was admitted to a psychiatric clinic for three weeks after he'd broken down at his workplace. As he noted earlier, those daily sessions with two therapists in November 2014 focussed solely on his work trauma. While talking brought a sense of relief, Jonathan says, without criticism, that it felt more like a debriefing of his high-profile cases than therapy.

'They were kind. And I was very grateful that they listened to me and understood. I could finally talk about the trauma I went through over all those years. It felt good to unburden myself. After two weeks they told me that I'd sacrificed enough for my country and that it was time to retire.'

Had Jonathan's therapists kept him in the clinic for the full three weeks and asked him about his personal life, they might have stumbled on the one unsolved case lurking like a monster in the shadows, quietly priming his ticking time-bomb. Instead the broken Confessor Cop was sent home with unspeakable grief wrapped up in an incomplete PTSD diagnosis.

'Do I think about my son? Almost every day. He was a funny, respectable guy and I loved him no matter what his circumstances were. He did not deserve to die that way. In fact, nobody deserves to die that way.'

Come October 2015, when Jonathan finally couldn't handle his job any more, he did not grasp how instrumental Cliffie's loss was in his leaving the cops. Just as he didn't grasp its import when our Sizzlers interviews triggered his PTSD days before Christmas 2021. Instead it would take Stephanie's startling revelation more than a decade after Cliffie's passing before Jonathan's stifled grief could tumble out and find its voice on these pages.

CHAPTER 23

I ATE MY BUS FARE

Jonathan's time-bomb started ticking in Philippi. Not during his baptism of fire as a rookie cop. Not when Greg and Goggie started stealing his bus fare in Standard 6. But as a five-year-old in 1964. In his own home.

It was a rented two-bedroom brick house with an outside toilet on Clear Water Farm, a Philippi smallholding located across Lansdowne Road from Nyanga East.

That's when his bricklayer father, Cyril, a serial philanderer, would return home drunk and beat up his mother, 28-year-old Elizabeth, who was four months pregnant with her fifth child, Wayne.

Jonathan's siblings, six-year-old Nigel, four-year-old Russell, and Beverley, aged two, stood by helplessly or fled to their shared bedroom, leaving it up to Jonathan, who had not yet started school, to restore law and order.

'I'd start crying, pleading with my parents to stop and get between them. But it made no difference. Ma couldn't keep quiet when the arguing started. She stood her ground and that made my father more angry. Then I would run to my Aunty Sarah, who lived nearby and beg her to come stop the fighting.'

Jonathan started Sub A at Myhof Primary in Lansdowne, emotionally distraught but always with a brave face.

'I was a nervous wreck.'

By the end of 1964, Jonathan, now six, was desperate.

'The abuse became unbearable. I couldn't take it any more. So I decided to stay with Aunty Agnes, my white family in Lansdowne, during the week and only go home on the weekends.'

It was usually safe then because his father's weekend womanising and drinking after playing goalkeeper for a Nyanga East soccer club kept him out of the house until the start of the new week. But to relocate to safety Jonathan had to hide his trauma from his aunt.

'If you started telling Aunty Agnes your problems she would put her hands over her ears. She was a woman of God who was allergic to any bad news. "Heavens!" she would say as soon as I started speaking. "No, no, no, my boy. I don't want to hear anything."

I just had to keep it to myself. So I ate my bus fare. I would catch the bus to school on Monday from Philippi, then buy a doughnut with my return fare.'

Jonathan would then walk to his aunt's house and tell her he had lost his bus fare.

Aunty Agnes must have suspected this was a ruse, that he was tacitly asking if he could stay at her house for the week. Or maybe she had been briefed by Jonathan's mother as to what was happening at home. He'll never know. To this day his ingenious survival strategy has never been discussed in the family. All that mattered to Jonathan then was that he had found a weekly refuge, a psychological fire escape. And that each Friday his Uncle Alex would usher him into his black VW Beetle and drive him home.

'Aunty Agnes's home was a happy home. There was no fighting. It was my safe place.'

Safe for the time being. No one in Jonathan's family had the skills to debrief the traumatised Morris siblings. Shame, too, kept it in the shadows. So Jonathan bottled up his pain and suffering. That's when his time-bomb was activated. And never detected. Not even by the therapists in 2014.

It explained why he leapfrogged these early childhood years in his biography document. The first time he would be able to look squarely at his early wounding was at the age of 65.

Once laptopping about Cliffie opened his emotional floodgates, he realised that the fear that had gagged him as a child no longer had the same hold over him. It was a courageous decision but in the final chapters the Confessor Cop knew *he* also had to make a confession.

Young Jonathan's itinerant lifestyle continued until early 1966, when his father moved out for good. Now in Standard 1, aged seven, he could return home safely each day.

Life returned to normal. At least for a while.

Then Cyril got wind that his ex-wife had taken a new lover 10 years her junior and was carrying this man's child. The lover, Paul Schmidt, was white, a railways maintenance worker, who had been living peacefully with his extended German family among their coloured Clear Water Farm neighbours.

According to the Immorality Act, Elizabeth and Paul were committing a crime. But the couple were planning to fly under the radar like Jonathan's light-skinned Uncle Alex, classified coloured even though his surname was Botha. He and Aunty Agnes, classified white, were quietly raising eight children in peace in nearby Lansdowne. In fact, they made a silent mockery of the system by registering five of Jonathan's cousins as white.

What Elizabeth and Paul hadn't anticipated was Cyril's jealous rage. And his sense of betrayal, as he had counted Paul a friend. Using a cruel political system that dehumanised him and his kin, Jonathan's father set the dogs of apartheid on the woman he had once vowed to love and cherish. Those dogs were the police. And when the police chased an Immorality Act case, they came late at night and banged loudly on the door. Which terrified and confused Jonathan.

In our discussions Jonathan remembered the police returning many times, loudly, often in the early hours of the morning, to catch his new father in bed with his mother.

'That pounding on the door would wake me from a deep sleep. Cops storming into the house and searching. Those were the scariest moments of my life. I was afraid that they would trap Paul. But my biggest fear was that they would arrest my mother or me.

Especially when she stood up to the cops. She didn't hold back. She'd shout at them. "What are you looking for? You've no right to be here!" I could see it made them edgy. They'd shout back, you're a cheeky woman. And she'd hit back. "It's my right to be cheeky in my own house."'

The cops' cat-and-mouse game turned Jonathan into a nervous wreck once more.

'I was always sleeping with one eye open, knowing the cops would be back. Paul was sharp. The cops never found him. But I was always fearful for his sake. Even on those nights he slept somewhere else. And even though they were hunting him, it felt like I was the one in hiding, waiting for the police to come and arrest me.'

Eventually Jonathan could take it no more and began eating his bus fare all over again. Two weeks before she was due, Elizabeth also fled to her family home in Idutywa in the Eastern Cape to remove any evidence from the apartheid crime scene. On 19 October 1966, she gave birth to Jennifer Schmidt there. Weeks later she was on the run again, this time to her mother in Durban, to settle her infant in her new home. A month later she returned to Clear Water. Alone.

Her broken heart was consoled by knowing that she had given her daughter a better life. A life free of further police harassment and even potential prosecution. The Immorality Act didn't just target couples. Children born to parents of different races were classified illegitimate by the state and were subject to additional racism, including loss of citizenship.

For a while Jonathan oscillated between Aunty Agnes and his mother until he was certain that the police raids had ceased.

'My father was the cause of the harassment. When he realised there was no hope that he and my mother would ever get together again, he stopped setting his police friends on my mom. He moved on with his life and left my mother in peace to have three more children with Paul.'

The next three years of Jonathan's life were happy. Beyond the blue gums surrounding the vegetable garden and pig hokkie at the back of his house, Jonathan and his Clear Water Farm buddies spun their wooden tops. They spent hours playing soccer, dominoes, marbles and kennetjie, which involved a player flipping a short stick into the air with a longer stick and then batting it to surrounding fielders.

He climbed and fell out of many trees, knowing he would get a hiding if he told his mother he had hurt himself. And he hunted laughing doves and braaied them because they tasted like chicken. Or he took them home for his mother to make her delicious bird soup.

But the game Jonathan loved most was cowboys-and-crooks played with guns made from sun-bleached sheep or cow jawbones and bullets fashioned from their teeth. Even as a kid, nothing could beat getting his man.

But come the end of 1969, the sudden selling of Clear Water had 11-year-old Jonathan on the move again. This time on a train to East London in a compartment crowded with his mother and six siblings, including new baby brothers, two-year-old Christopher and eight-month-old Jerome.

Aunty Viola's three-bedroom house in East London was already bursting with five of Jonathan's cousins and three boarders. But her generous soul made room for them all while Paul built a pondok in Lourdes, a growing informal settlement on Lansdowne Road just three bus stops from Clear Water.

Overcrowding and lack of privacy were the last things on Jonathan's mind. 'We were small and didn't take up a lot of space. We were comfortable. And there were playmates everywhere. I was never lonely or anxious. It was just never-ending fun.'

Seeing this and knowing Viola loved her son like one of her own, Elizabeth enrolled him and younger brother Russell at AWS Barnes Primary before leaving with the rest of her brood for their new home in Lourdes.

Initially Jonathan struggled with Standard 5. But with help from his cousins and his aunt, a teacher at his school, he ended the year with a 70% pass rate. After class he played soccer and rugby and turned out to be his school's fastest sprinter. Until interschools, he notes, when the Indian kids from neighbouring schools 'het my deurmekaar gehardloop'.

The fast-maturing 12-year-old ended one of the best years of his childhood with a sense of belonging and worthiness.

'And peace. There was no conflict.'

This was largely thanks to Aunty Viola, a deeply spiritual woman who would one day keep her favourite nephew safe in her prayers while carefully cutting newspaper articles about his cases to tuck them away somewhere between Matthew, Mark, Luke and John.

Come the year-end Jonathan couldn't wait to get back to Cape Town. But his optimism was misplaced. Unable to enrol 12-year-old Jonathan at her first-choice school, Oaklands High, his mother chose Silverstream in nearby Manenberg. 'From the very first day I had a gut feeling that I wasn't safe,' says Jonathan, recalling how he handed his expensive Rotary watch, a gift from Paul, to his mother as she left after introductions in the principal's office. 'I knew if I kept it, I'd be robbed.'

It didn't help. For the rest of Standard 6, Greg and Goggie ambushed Jonathan almost every day to steal his bus fare before he could even consider eating it. 'I sat with fear in class. I didn't know which way to turn. I was a nervous wreck all over again.'

Jonathan's trauma time-bomb ticked away wildly for the rest of the year until he decided he had had enough.

Changing schools helped. Until Greg showed up again and 13-year-old Jonathan exploded with rage. His risky, impulsive behaviour against a dangerous adult gangster twice his age wasn't just David defeating Goliath. It was also a classic red flag of untreated trauma, according to experts like psychiatrist Dr Bessel van der Kolk and psychologist Dr Peter Levine, both pioneering researchers of childhood trauma and its untreated outcomes.

The red flag showed itself again as Jonathan's Dirty Harry.

For Constable Morris, taking the law into his own hands might have been a way of dealing with an immediate problem but it also meant risking a fledgling career. In another sense it was an unconscious way of regulating childhood trauma.

There was also no solace in coming home to Lourdes, a squatter camp that bore no resemblance to its namesake French village famed for miracle healings. With five siblings already squeezed into one room of the two-roomed shack, Jonathan and Russell had to make do with a shared single bed in the kitchen. Their clothes were stored in suitcases under their bed. They washed in a steel bath that was the source of many a squabble over who went next. From a communal tap 30 metres away, the siblings took turns carrying water in buckets that were warmed on a woodburning, cast-iron Welcome Dover stove. And they fought over whose turn it was on the chore list to clean the outside bucket toilet.

At first, living in a shack with its leaky roof in the bush in a rapidly growing informal settlement didn't bother Jonathan. 'We had shoes on our feet, a roof over our head and food on the table. We were poor but happy.'

But it began to weigh on the growing teenager who still carried the shame of how his mother had been abused. 'I had nice friends at school. But they all stayed close to one another in decent houses in Wetton. I was too embarrassed to invite them to my pondok. Especially the girls I liked.'

For a while the 15-year-old held his shame close. Spending far too much time on his own, he escaped now and then up a dilapidating nine-metre church tower built in 1922 by a resident Irish priest. 'It was nice to clean my head up there. To feel free like a bird in the sky. I would spend hours enjoying the view and building light castles in the air about the day I'd become a rich man who would take his family out of poverty.'

Down on the ground there was no daydreaming as soon as the 16-year-old schoolboy was thrust prematurely into adulthood.

'Paul was struggling to make ends meet. By the time I dropped out at the end of Standard 8, Nigel was already working. But the family needed my support as well. I couldn't expect Paul to buy my clothes or support me any more.'

For a while Jonathan found solace in his job and his jolling teenage relationships. But dating away from home soon brought its own complications as he battled to sustain any intimate connection with the mothers of the two sons he fathered while still a teenager.

It was the start of Jonathan's struggle to form healthy, secure attachments in relationships. Another classic sign of unresolved trauma, this pattern repeated itself for decades until Jonathan came to rest with his wife Leonore.

The trauma literature calls this pattern 'repetition compulsion' or 'trauma reenactment'.

'Here's one of the more unusual and problem-creating symptoms that can develop from unresolved trauma: the compulsion to repeat the actions that caused the problem in the first place,' writes Dr Peter Levine in *Healing Trauma: Restoring the Wisdom of Your Body*. 'We are inextricably drawn into situations that replicate the original trauma in both obvious and less obvious ways. The prostitute or stripper with a history of childhood sexual abuse is a common example.

'Reenactments may be played out in intimate relationships, work situations, repetitive accidents or mishaps, and in other seemingly random events. They may also appear in the form of bodily symptoms or psychosomatic diseases.'

Levine explains that trauma, especially childhood trauma, leaves an individual stuck in a state of fight, flight or freeze. Reenactment is the body's way – almost always unconsciously – of trying to return to the state of equilibrium it was in before the trauma occurred.

Put another way, by mimicking the traumatic situation either symbolically or literally, individuals are attempting to complete the body's unfinished responses to resolve the trauma. This repetition didn't just play itself out unconsciously in Jonathan's relationships with the mothers of his children, but in his career as well. It seems to be the only plausible explanation for him becoming a cop.

Why else would the teenager sign up to the ranks of those who cruelly and profoundly abused him and his family when he was a little boy? Why else would he don the uniform of the scariest moments of his life? The uniform that invoked so much fear that he became a nervous seven-year-old wreck?

At first the Mongrels challenged Jonathan's trauma reenactments, which nearly ended his rookie Philippi days. But he found equilibrium as he honed his detective craft. The crime would mimic the trauma he felt as a child. Then he'd play his favourite childhood game, cowboys-and-crooks, and soothe his trauma by getting his man – quickly.

And round and round he went, ironically adding more violent trauma as he tried to resolve his original trauma with law and order. Until his workaholic treadmill that had served him so well broke – in the wake of the cruel death of his second son, whose birth marked Jonathan's genesis as a cop.

In essence, getting his man was Jonathan's adult way of eating his bus fare. Which is why the Confessor Cop panicked when he couldn't solve Sizzlers in his customary 48 hours. It was his unconscious alarm bell that his trauma time-bomb was still ticking.

This, too, explains his meltdown in December 2021, after one too many reenactments of the horror on Graham Road. I was retraumatising him all over again. Reminding him in the process that his brilliant survival strategy was flawed.

And then the miraculous happened. Detective Captain Morris, looking for a breakthrough in his unconscious self, stumbled on laptop therapy. As any good detective would. Laptopping became his new reenactment strategy. His most novel and brilliant way yet of eating his bus fare.

CHAPTER 24

MA

By the end of 1978, the newly graduated cop was gatvol of shack life. So when his cousin offered him a room in his Mitchells Plain flat, he jumped at it. But within a year he was on the move again. His living conditions had improved but the pattern of his life was the same.

He fell in love with Hanover Park typist Shireen, married her and moved into Aunt Edna's house in Bellville South. Then he was off to a friend's smallholding on Klipfontein Mission Station, where his beautiful bundle of joy, Natasha, was born in March 1980. He was 21.

Then Lady Luck smiled. Coloured cops didn't qualify for a SAP housing loan. That was for whites only, but a sergeant at the Philippi Police Station had a sister who was selling houses. She had a way to wangle a R8,000 bond. And for that he got a brand-new three-bedroom house in the new Mitchells Plain suburb of Port-lands, in a street called Bulawayo Close.

It was big. With a big lounge and a big yard. Too big for his small family of three. But that's not why Jonathan bought his first house. This was for his mother, Paul, and his siblings, who could not believe their ears when he told them. This was the manifestation of a solemn promise to himself to lead his family out of poverty.

To this day, he considers this to be the greatest achievement of his life. And he managed to pull it off before he had turned 22, while in the process of learning fast that being a policeman was not child's play.

Jonathan knew then, without a shadow of a doubt, that you didn't need a big bank balance to feel like the wealthiest man alive. His joy over Ma's face when he finally surprised her is one of his enduring memories. Another is his mother walking down Bulawayo Close with the estate agent, sling bag over her shoulder, as if she were the wealthiest woman in the world. The street of houses was so new that Ma was able to choose the one she really wanted. She picked house number nine.

Jonathan remembers the joyful hugs and shared tears of gratitude. The sheer delight. The unforgettable explosion of joy in his heart. He had found a safe haven for Ma. One he could also return to.

Indeed, he and Shireen moved into that house with his mother when Natasha was just a few months old. He wanted to feel the happiness of his family in the new house. And it was just like old times. Beverley, Wayne, Christopher, Jerome and Carl squeezed happily into one room again to make space for his family. The difference this time was that the roof didn't leak and there were no arguments about fetching water, nor was there an outside bucket toilet to clean. And Ma had a newborn to love like her own.

Eighteen months later, Jonathan was on the move again, this time into a two-bedroom flat in Woodlands just in time for the early New Year birth of Simone. But eventually, in the swirl of raising two babies, the detective's trauma reenactments on the beat started to affect his young family's happiness.

'I was still young and full of energy, working long hours and partying with colleagues until the early hours of the morning,' explains Jonathan. 'It didn't sit well with Shireen. She began verbally abusing me. Then it started getting physical. It was embarrassing going to work with scratch marks on my face.'

It was also traumatising. 'The fighting and shouting reminded me of my childhood years.'

Eight years into their marriage, the couple attempted a trial separation in the hope of reconciliation. But it ended in divorce. Fortunately, not an acrimonious one. They remained good friends and Jonathan didn't abandon his children, fetching and carrying them to and from school. When his work schedule could no longer cope with this, he gave his Opel Rekord to Shireen, who had moved on with a new husband.

'Are you mad?' asked his colleagues when they saw the new man behind the wheel.

'This is not about me', he told them. 'This is about my children.'

He missed them terribly. When drowning his sorrows while partying, he always ended up singing Wayne Newton's country ballad 'Daddy Don't You Walk So Fast'.

'They were always on my mind. The only problem was I didn't turn back home.'

Instead, he returned to Ma's place to lick his wounds.

The same scene would repeat itself 16 years later with Sizzlers and a soon-to-be-ex-wife arguing with him.

'The verbal abuse was far worse than in my first marriage. And the divorce was messy because it was all about money. But once it was done, it was done. We never communicated again.'

Jonathan had no memory of Leonore when she was the pastor's wife in number eight, Bulawayo Close. They were in the only other occupied home on the Close when his mother made her choice but, by the time he returned there in 2003, Leonore had been gone from the street for 12 years. However, she kept in touch with Jonathan's mother and was a frequent visitor. Indeed, Elizabeth and Leonore had quickly bonded from the start while Ma was setting up house and had become firm friends.

Eventually in 2010, Jonathan began dating Leonore secretly and quickly realised this woman was the one he could finally come home to. He had found his safe haven.

His mother's house bore witness to a number of life-altering events.

There was, his sister, Jennifer's joyful return in June 1983, a year-and-a-half after the birth of Simone. She was 17 when Elizabeth went to Durban to fetch her. Jonathan still remembers the picture of happiness as they alighted from the train at Cape Town station. 'Ma was smiling from ear to ear. They held each other close all the way home.'

Buying his own house in Westridge soon after divorcing Shireen was another highlight. But after just two years he was on the move again, this time to his new girlfriend's house in Portlands. The Westridge house he gave to his newlywed siblings so that they had a decent place to stay while they found their feet. Love and generosity were qualities he'd inherited from his mother.

But it wasn't all wine and roses back at Ma's place. Just before Jonathan moved away in March 1989, he heard from his brothers that a drunken Paul had hit their mother during an argument. Once he had sobered up the next morning, Paul packed his bags and left.

Jonathan's immediate reaction was sadness. His mother, now 53, did not deserve another abusive relationship. She had earned a peaceful life.

As Paul had left, Jonathan convinced his angry brothers to let matters lie. Elizabeth, as loving as she was, could also be stubborn. Paul had crossed a line. She would never take him back.

Elizabeth eventually told Jonathan the arguments with Paul had been escalating for some time. To Jonathan, Paul had always been loving and caring. Had always loved Elizabeth dearly. He had always been a good provider to them all. A good father. There was never such a thing as step-brothers and -sisters. But when it came to Ma, possessiveness and jealousy were his downfall.

For Jonathan, Paul's violence triggered memories of his father's violence. At the time he wasn't as aware of his own trauma as he is now, so he did what he did best before he found laptopping. He pushed it down. Bottled it up. At the time, neither he nor his mother had the words or the understanding to address the hurt they had suffered throughout their lives.

The following year, 1990, the family suffered the tragedy of brother Russell's drowning, two weeks before Christmas. But life went on. The years went by. Elizabeth endured until at the age of 80 she suffered a heart attack that scared her family. But it needed more than a heart attack to take the old lady down.

Ma returned to her home and for the next five years was fully self-sufficient, still doing her own housework and ruling her roost. She was the family's dancing queen, jiving the night away on her 85th birthday to Master KG's 'Jerusalema' and other favourites.

That's how Jonathan remembers her until just before Easter 2021, when a serious stroke put his mother back into frail care. But not for long. The family wanted her to pass her last weeks peacefully back home where they could love and care for her.

She'd already made peace with her husbands. Cyril in the late-1980s, when he repeatedly asked for forgiveness. By the time he died in 2006, bygones were bygones.

Paul started making amends three weeks before Elizabeth's death. He came several times to pray at her bedside. With her sons he would be one of her pallbearers.

When Ma sensed the end was not far off, she summonsed the family and her favourite church band. This occurred during the Covid lockdown, so her neighbours could not have attended her funeral anyhow.

Instead, wearing her royal-blue gown and with a blanket across her legs, she said goodbye from her wheelchair. Royal blue was her favourite colour, similar in colour to the dress Jonathan had bought for her the previous Christmas. Ma was a well-dressed woman who never wore the same dress to a function. It was an affordable indulgence, remarked Jennifer in her eulogy, because Jonathan was Ma's ATM. He enjoyed that role. He would never be able to pay her back for what she had done for her family.

On this farewell occasion, her son, Wayne, pushed the wheelchair as the brass band, dressed in red and black, led the procession down Bulawayo Close. Ma paused at each gate for a final farewell.

'Hello, Aunty Cupie,' neighbours called from their garden gates. They hadn't seen her since she'd been bedridden.

'Goodbye, Aunty Cupie!'

'All the best, Aunty Cupie!'

'She gave them the royal wave,' chuckles Jonathan.

For the rest of that sunny Sunday afternoon, the band belted out more hymns from under the blue gazebo in Ma's yard. From her wheelchair, she sang and clapped along. The neighbours joined in. It was like church. How she had missed her Sundays at Westridge church with Pastor Greg on the pulpit. It went on for hours. And Ma was the life of the party one last time.

In the week that followed she went blind and could no longer talk. Sister Beverley, who lived with Ma, alerted her siblings that it was time. Jonathan arrived in the early evening of 9 June to spend some time alone with his mother.

Ma had no favourites. She loved all her children fiercely and equally. But Jonathan was her closest.

'I think the bond between us was much tighter than the other siblings. Knowing and remembering the abuse she went through in my childhood years made me over-protective towards her.'

Other family who knew this were worried about how Jonathan would cope with her death. They were on hand, watching just in case.

Jonathan lay with his head on his mother's bosom. By now she was weak, her one arm already lame. He placed it gently on his head and wept. Almost silently. Those outside could not hear. But it was so visceral he struggled to breathe.

In between he spoke the same four words.

'I love you, Ma.'

'I love you, Ma.' Over and over again.

All Ma could do was nod her head until it was time to go.

CHAPTER 25

LOST AND FOUND

Jonathan couldn't stick around for Ma's last breath. He left his sisters to hold a mirror close to their mother's mouth to make certain she wasn't breathing before calling the funeral parlour.

He asked his niece, Nicolette, to call him when they knew. He didn't want sister Beverley to phone because, although she had taken care of her mother through this time, he knew she would cry and then he would too. He waited up through the long night until his phone rang in the early morning.

'Uncle Jonathan...'

He didn't let Nicolette finish. 'Is Ma gone?'

'Yes.'

'Thank you. I'm on my way.'

He was so sad. But also grateful Ma's suffering was over.

She has been gone several years now. But her absence is still an ache. He misses the long daily conversations. The ambling Sunday drives. Her jokes. Funny stories about her childhood mischief. He misses popping into number nine unexpectedly.

To soothe his ache, Jonathan watches phone videos of Ma dancing, ululating with joy. But the videos don't help when conversation strays carelessly to those last tender hours with her. During telephone conversations I have with Jonathan, talking about his mother is the only time he weeps. Imperceptibly, because he swallows the sobbing. Then immediately rings off to release his grief alone.

The moment she died he was on his own. There would be no more returning to Ma in an unconscious attempt to heal those early wounds, to regulate his unresolved trauma. The lost-boy-wounds. It was time to go home to himself. To learn how to reassure his inner self. He couldn't verbalise it at the time, but this unconscious inner knowing was freaking him out when our interviews for his memoir dragged him back into the Sizzlers house in 2021. This lasted until that near-Christmas bombshell WhatsApp saying it was too much, when he pleaded for us to stop.

He felt as if he was going to die, he said. Opening up Sizzlers came too soon after Ma's death. A mere six months after the gospel band followed the hearse out of Bulawayo Close, past neighbours weeping at their gates.

He missed her so much. The grief also brought flashbacks of those Sizzlers boys that were as vivid as his first hesitant entrance into that room in 2003. Then came his first Christmas without Ma's chicken and roast potatoes. Christmas when the family still missed Russell.

He only revealed all this as we were putting the finishing words to his memoir.

'I don't deal well with sympathy. That's why I kept it to myself.'

Until Ma left. She might not have been able to talk about Jonathan's trauma, but her parting gift was to turn his conversation inward. And in so doing she gifted her son with his most profound and private investigation of his life.

There is a school of thought that views trauma as incomplete childhood learning. It explains why similar events that might traumatise one person do not impact another. Transcending trauma, according to this model, occurs through a relearning.

Learning is complete, says one expert, when you have properly understood and contextualised the sequence of traumatic events. And also integrated the emotional impact of them. You need to be an adult before this can happen. You don't have the understanding as a child.

This has been Jonathan's redemption road. A road he will travel until it's time to join Ma.

As the detective's self-examination continued, some clues were in plain sight, others hidden. For instance, there's the serial killer who shared the detective's initials. Was it also pure coincidence that the Jesus Killer found God while writing his confessional letters in the early hours in the quiet solitude of his cell? Was this when the seed for Jonathan's laptopping method were sown subconsciously, when he read Jimmy Maketta's extraordinary letters?

Was it also pure accident that the Sizzlers case that tipped Jonathan over the edge was littered with lost boys? Lost boys living in poverty. In one room as overcrowded as Clear Water, Aunty Viola's house, or Lourdes. Out of suitcases doubling as cupboards. Far away from their mothers. Mothers oblivious of their pain. Gagged, silenced as little Jonathan was when he couldn't talk about the abuse of Ma. The police hounding Ma. His fear.

The truth is Ma had to die to set her son free. For it was only then that the hidden truths revealed themselves. Yet he expressed his concern to me that he had exposed too much of himself in these pages.

How would the family react to his truth? The truth about Ma? Some might prefer to forget.

But we all know the truth. Don't live with the hurt. The truth sets you free.

Clear your heart, Jonathan, because it's healing.

Tell it like it is, Jonathan.

Tell it like it is.

ABOUT THE AUTHOR

Capetonian Michael Behr has been a newspaper journalist and magazine features writer for local and international titles for four decades. He has won a number of Mondi Paper Magazine Awards for his feature writing, including a finalist award in 2003 for Ghetto Defendant, his exclusive, penetrating profile of former Springbok wing Ashwin Willemse. Published in Sports Illustrated, it was later reprinted as a case study in the academic setwork Writing for the Media in Southern Africa.

In 2014, he published his first book, Call It Like It Is – the best-selling memoir of legendary rugby referee Jonathan Kaplan.

That same year, his behind-the-scenes coverage of the honeymoon murder of Anni Dewani produced a series of UK front-page scoops. His subsequent coverage of several more high-profile murder trials regularly made headlines in South African weekend papers.

This prepared him for his first foray into film in 2021, when he joined an award-winning UK production company as the South African producer of a true-crime documentary on the Dewani saga for the Discovery+ channel.

In 2025, he assisted in the production of another Dewani murder documentary – this time for Amazon – due to be released at the end of the year.